FIRST

The Moral, Social and
Religious Challenges of the Day

FIRST THINGS

The Moral, Social and Religious Challenges of the Day

CHARLES MOORE
GYLES BRANDRETH
CHERIE BOOTH
GEORGE WEIGEL

Published in association with the Tyburn Community

BURNS & OATES
A Continuum imprint
LONDON • NEW YORK

Burns & Oates
A Continuum imprint
The Tower Building, 11 York Road, London SE1 7NX
15 East 26th Street, New York, NY 10010

www.continuumbooks.com

First published 2005

British Library Cataloguing-in-Publication Data
A catalogue record for this book is available from the British Library.

ISBN 0 8601 2388 X

Designed and typeset by Kenneth Burnley, Wirral, Cheshire
Printed and bound in Great Britain by MPG Books Ltd,
Bodmin, Cornwall

Contents

Foreword

The gallows at Tyburn – a site sometimes disputed, but now thought to have lain on the south-east side of Connaught Square, near Marble Arch – was the favoured site for London hangings for almost six hundred years. The first unfortunate victim, William Longbeard, was hanged there in 1196; the last, John Austen, in 1783. From 1531 to the final decades of the seventeenth century, during the period of religious strife and upheaval that followed Henry VIII's break with Rome, and which propelled Britain into the heart of the European Protestant Reformation, some 105 Roman Catholics were executed at Tyburn for their faith, often in the cruellest and most protracted manner.

The annual Tyburn lecture, established in 2001, commemorates, by its name, the execution of those Catholic martyrs, done to death, as Cherie Booth says, by a State that claimed the right to regulate the conscience of the individual and to impose religious allegiance and uniformity on everyone. But it also represents the contribution that the Catholic Church in Britain has made, and continues to make, to the wider society of which it is part.

As the Archbishop of Westminster, Cardinal Cormac Murphy O'Connor, has said, 'It is important that the Catholic community contributes to the public life and discourse of our country, especially in relation to the moral, religious and social challenges of the day.' The Tyburn lectures, now in their fifth year, are designed to help the Church fulfil that important role.

This volume, publishing in full, for the first time, the texts of the four lectures that have been delivered to date, shows how varied the response to ongoing debates, across a wide range of subjects, can be.

Charles Moore draws fully on his experience as a journalist and former editor of the *Daily Telegraph* to consider the ever-pressing need for independence, fearlessness and plain speaking in public life. Gyles Brandreth outlines a manifesto for the reinvention of childhood, which recognizes and protects the innocence of children while helping them to adapt to ever-changing needs of the twenty-first-century world. Cherie Booth speaks, from her vantage point as one of this country's leading human-rights lawyers, of the need for the vision of equality before God to be reflected in our legal systems, and of the important part that the Catholic Church can play in eradicating all social or cultural discrimination. Finally, George Weigel, the distinguished Catholic theologian and intellectual, offers a challenging redefinition of the relevance of the Church's social doctrine to a free and virtuous society.

In the brief period since their inception, the Tyburn annual lecture has established itself as an event that commands wide attention and has very considerable influence. This book explains why.

Rt Hon Michael Ancram QC MP
December 2004

1

CHARLES MOORE

Witness to the Truth

WHEN I SAT DOWN to write this, the first Tyburn lecture, I found myself in the frame of mind which Dr Johnson famously observed. 'Depend upon it, sir,' he told Boswell, 'when a man knows he is to be hanged the next morning, it concentrates his mind wonderfully.'

Too many of the men invited to address an audience at Tyburn have found that those words have been their last. And therefore, although it is a great honour to be asked to give this lecture, it is even more terrifying than it would be to give a lecture anywhere else.

The history of Tyburn is grim indeed. From 1196 to 1783, it was the main place of execution in London, and there seems to have been very little dignity, and sometimes very little justice, in the show put on here. As he and his fellows were about to die a few yards from this spot Edmund Campion exclaimed, '*Spectaculum facti sumus Deo, angelis et hominibus!*' – 'We are made a spectacle to God, His angels and to men!' And a spectacle the thing was, over the centuries, with its grandstands and its mob, its vendors of gin and ballads and oranges, its superstitions about the medicinal properties of the dead man's hand, and the privileges of the hangman, who adjourned to the pub afterwards and sold off sections of the fatal rope for sixpence a piece.

It might, at first sight, seem extraordinary that such a place should be chosen for a religious order to live and pray, a place from which God seems so distant. There is often, indeed, a curious blasphemy about the rituals surrounding executions. 'When the condemned men set off to Tyburn from Newgate prison, they were handed nosegays by women known as "the frail sisterhood"', prostitutes standing in the shadow of the Church of the Holy Sepulchre there. In a sort of parodied communion, they drank ritual jugs of ale outside St Giles-in-the-Fields. As if in imitation of the three crucifixes at Golgotha, the triangular scaffold was known as 'the triple tree'. And rather as, in the New Testament, people cast lots for Christ's vesture, at Tyburn the executioner could sell the dead man's garment. At Tyburn in 1447 five men had already been hanged, cut down while still alive and marked out for quartering when their pardon arrived. The hangman let them free, but forced them to go naked so that he could keep their clothes.

In short, most of what happened at Tyburn displayed humanity at its most base – cruel, greedy, unjust, mocking. Why should Christians seek out such a place?

The answer, of course, is that a religion of the Incarnation cannot avoid humankind at its worst, the moments when the agonies and defects of the flesh are most real. The reason there is a convent at Tyburn is the same reason that there is representation of a man hanging from a cross in every Church. Indeed, it is a particularly impressive aspect of Christianity that its followers feel called to holiness by such grim places when others might shun them. When I visited Tokyo, for example, I found that what was once the public execution ground was now home to members of the untouchable caste, all of them poor and some destitute. It was no surprise to find that the main ministry to them was from the Missionaries of Charity of Mother Teresa.

But the particular aspect of Tyburn which prompts my thoughts is that of martyrdom, or rather, of what the word martyr, in the original Greek, means – witness.

The idea of witness is inseparable from a revealed and proselytizing religion. If you have been given the truth, you must bear witness to it. By my count, there are 178 occasions in the Bible when the word 'witness' is used, the great majority of them in the New Testament. And it is partly through witnessing the ultimate act of witness, which is martyrdom, that others bear witness in their turn. St Paul, at that time called Saul, looked after the robes of the men who stoned Stephen, and supported their action. What he witnessed helped to lead him towards conversion. Here at Tyburn, Henry Walpole found his coat splashed by the blood of Campion as he was disembowelled, and was inspired by what he witnessed to martyrdom himself 13 years later.

Witness to the truth is not only a duty upon the faithful: it is a necessity for the functioning of any remotely decent society. No respectable legal system, for example, can do without witnesses. It was a point that Campion made at his trial when faced with unsupported accusations. 'The wisdom and providence of the laws of England . . . is such as proceedeth not to the trial of any man for life or death by shifts of probabilities and conjectural surmises, without proof of the crime by sufficient evidence and substantial witness.' Such proof was never offered, but, by the paradox of martyrdom, the injustice of his trial enabled Campion to bear witness of a higher kind.

The problem I want to discuss is the problem of witness to the truth in Britain today.

None of us, thank goodness, is called in Britain nowadays to anything like what so many suffered at Tyburn. One does not have to be a believer in the Whig interpretation of history, in the notion of perpetual progress towards ever greater freedom and civilization, to feel that some lessons have been learnt between now and 1581. We must be grateful for our almost unique national continuity which allows us today to use the very words which Campion used and to speak of 'Elizabeth, your Queen and my Queen', but we should also give thanks for the fact that today none of us has our loyalty challenged at the price of our life. All we are expected to do is to turn up on polling day and put a cross beside the candidate we would prefer, thus making our contribution to that Queen's Government. And even that simple action is not compulsory. As crosses go, it is a light one to bear.

I genuinely believe that this state of affairs, this lightness of being, is preferable to the world which Campion knew. Those religious people who seek a return to persecution in order to produce greater faith are like those who seek war in order to promote courage – they display a frivolity about what is actually involved. The blood of the martyrs may be the seed of the Church, but that does not justify us in seeking to shed it. Martyrdom is justified only when it is necessary. When it is not, it is fanatical and callous, as one sees with the terrible fate of suicide bombers and their victims in Israel.

But it is undoubtedly true that special difficulties are created for witness in a society when the cost of belief seems so low. If we are not threatened by 'dungeon, fire and sword', will we ever bother to test what we do believe and answer the demands of that belief? The sobering answer is, probably not.

Do the liberal tolerance and prosperity of our society – both, in my view, thoroughly good things in themselves – nevertheless allow us to be led away from what we think we believe? For example, the Left has been very effective in ridiculing and undermining the demands of monotheistic religion in relation to sex. The Right has done a no-less-successful job in relation to money. To challenge either of these is to invite ridicule; to give in to them involves no very obvious suffering nor blatant wickedness. Even the tolerance of the differing views of others – one of the best and most overdue developments of twentieth-century Christianity – has its temptations. I have read Mr Blair saying, for instance, that he opposes abortion, but he has never voted against it because he does not think that his views should be 'imposed' on women. If he were speaking of contraception, such a view would be defensible, but the whole point about abortion from the view of its opponents is that no one – not even a mother – should have the right of life and death over another. Thus the liberal Mr Blair is helping to 'impose' something more absolute than a mere opinion upon unborn children. There is no reason to doubt that he is sincere in his disapproval of abortion, but the compromise he has made with secular society means that, objectively, he is assisting it. We are almost all of us, to greater or lesser degrees, guilty of comparable collusions.

Let me say a bit more about this in relation to public affairs and what I see in the work which I find myself doing every day.

As well as being a former place of execution, Tyburn was an underground stream. It used to empty in St James's Park and find its way at last, via the Old Ditch and the Marflete, into the Thames. I once worked literally and I still work figuratively in the place named after another dishonoured and dirty river, Fleet Street. The Fleet used to carry butchers' offal and other garbage downstream, and it is at least poetically appropriate that for 300 years this ditch has been associated with journalism. As the *London Encyclopaedia* succinctly puts it, 'The Fleet is still a sewer.' Many victims of the British press would agree. Journalism is a powerful tributary flowing into the great river of our national life, and not a very clean one.

Having edited one national title or another – with one short break – since 1984, I have witnessed a considerable change in the conduct of public affairs. This is expressed in words like 'accountability', 'transparency' and 'openness'. Because people believe more and more seriously that no one has a God-given right to exercise authority over anyone else, they demand a constant scrutiny of all those who hold public positions. Because the history of the last hundred years has made us more horribly aware than ever of the abuse of power, we hedge it about.

Thus it is that businesses spend a vast amount of time on corporate compliance, that the police have to confront accusations of being 'institutionally racist', that the army has to think about the rights of women and homosexuals in its ranks, instead of devoting all its energies to working out what it needs to fight. Under Mr Major's administration, Parliament decided that it did not trust itself to behave ethically, and so set up the Nolan Committee. Peerages now have to be awarded by a semi-public procedure (although one notices that exactly the same sort of people end up wearing ermine). Would-be bishops of the Church of England may soon have to present CVs and fill in application forms, going against the ancient principle that no one who thinks he should be a bishop is suitable to be one. Admissions to universities or the Civil Service have to be conducted according to examinable procedures. Even people who wish to give their time gratis for public service, such as by being a trustee of a museum or an art gallery, must fill in forms and answer tricky questions. Even the intelligence services have to go to court – and may well lose – when they seek to defend the secrecy on which their work depends. The Queen pays tax. The Lord Chancellor has to answer for his wallpaper.

So much of this is good. Grotesque abuses of power are harder to conceal in modern society than in the past. The trend to openness often exposes the indefensibility of those who resist it. It is ever-more obviously scandalous, for example, that the meetings of the Council of Ministers which is, in effect, the EU's law-making body, take place behind closed doors. It has become much harder nowadays to defend a National Health Service which gives the patient so little information and so much delay. Public service is invigilated, and so it should be.

But there is a cost, and it is paid in the area of witness. In my years as an Editor, I have noticed a decline – almost a collapse – of public figures who are prepared to be publicly brave. If you are constantly subject to a scrutiny which tends to see you as guilty unless you are proved innocent, you will become more and more risk-averse. If you are always having to look over your shoulder, you cannot look forward.

Who can you think of, in our public life today, who says anything so strongly and boldly that you can remember it afterwards? Who in senior public positions believes that he or she will get the necessary support if he tries to do or say anything that is difficult? Where are the prophetic voices? Who are our Florence Nightingale or Matthew Arnold or John Ruskin or J. M. Keynes or Cobden or Wilberforce or Cobbett? Who, even, are the

Margaret Thatchers or Aneurin Bevans active in contemporary politics?

For a senior policeman or a general or the chairman of a public company or a Cabinet minister or the Director-General of the BBC or a bishop or a vice-chancellor or a judge or a head teacher, the chief note of public utterance is defensive. Not for nothing is the phrase 'damage limitation' a coinage of our times.

I can certainly think of eloquent voices saying something today which, whether right or wrong, is worth hearing. There is Sir David Ramsbotham drawing attention to what he sees as the scandalous state of our prisons. There is Chris Woodhead, proclaiming the failure of our schools. There is the Prince of Wales standing up for all values in life which are sacrificed by the obsession with profit and mere functionality. All brave voices. But it is noticeable that such people are in positions which are not primarily executive. Those who are tend more than ever to keep their heads down. And when those heads do reluctantly pop up over the parapet it is usually to say that they 'take on board' the criticisms that have been made or that they are 'in listening mode'. Too often nowadays a public career is an unappealing mixture of obscurity and humiliation.

I was much struck by a phrase in an article which we published in the *Daily Telegraph* by Bob Kiley, the American with the admirable but almost Icarus-like ambition to get the London Underground working. He complained of what he called 'the post-modern obsession of avoiding responsibility'. He is right.

We may all agree that power should be diffused and that decisions should be called to account. But if the buck stops nowhere, two things happen. The first is that somewhere, secretly, deviously, power does, in fact, operate. So, for example, a world in which the police dare not arrest people is a world in which other, nastier people – criminals – exercise a far more arbitrary authority. The second is that the buck-passers are failing and being encouraged to fail in one of the great human duties – bearing witness to the truth. Bob Kiley calls this post-modern, and to be post-modern, surely, is to be post-Christian. Whether Protestant or Catholic, the Christian has an overwhelming duty to his conscience. His conscience informs him of his responsibilities and therefore reproaches him when he avoids them. The idea of a conscience is far too un-ironic for the post-modern mind. If you have no inner voice to answer to, you will feel perfectly at ease if you merely manage to get on, keep your nose clean and collect your pension. Your conscience tells you that you *must* do or say something. The post-modern mind knows no such imperative.

In this state of affairs, something worse than inertia and timidity can set in.

Those who seek to exploit the culture of accountability can do so. Litigation can be used to paralyse an institution. So can false accusations. Take the difficulties that now beset all those institutions, including the Church, which have the care of children. We seem to have moved, in a frighteningly short time, from an era in which some teachers or priests got away with outrageous abuses of children because no one could question their authority, to one in which any teacher or priest lives in daily danger of having his career ruined by the witch-hunters of child abuse. The damage done to innocent professionals is obvious. Perhaps less obvious, but equally important, is the damage done to young children who are taught not to trust and will never know the physical touch of a loving teacher or pastor because it is actually forbidden by this zealotry. An atmosphere of fear and suspicion prevails. Those in authority become more preoccupied with self-protecting procedures than with the needs of the children they serve, and power shifts to the 'whistle-blower' who, once indefensibly ignored, is now overindulged. 'Whistle-blowers' are sometimes brave witnesses to the truth: sometimes they are no more than grudge-bearers.

Where does all this leave my own trade? Uncomfortably close to the centre of the action, I think.

At its best, journalism is a rough-and-ready, day-by-day, common-or-garden version of the witness to the truth which is required of us all. Such journalism tries hard to tell readers accurately what has just happened. When you consider the often acute shortage of time available in which to ascertain the facts, I think the daily newspapers do this job surprisingly well. Most days, most of the broadsheet papers will summarize and depict fairly accurately the chief events in the nation and the world, as well as furnishing a mass of other information – sport results, market prices, weather forecasts – in a comprehensible shape. In addition, they will analyse, argue, describe and amuse. This is not bad for the third of the price of an espresso coffee at Starbucks. Without us, people would know much less of the world in which they live. It is impossible for anyone wishing to establish a tyranny to avoid taking control of the press, which is another way of saying that a free press such as ours is bound to be, in part at least, a true one. Anyone who does not want people to bear witness to the truth must muzzle the press.

And of course our function as witness goes further than this. We are not only the regurgitator of information about public affairs: we are also its critic. Explicitly, we claim to expose untruth or wrongdoing. Implicitly, we pass judgement on the information received by deciding whether or not to publish it, and what prominence we should give it. Newspapers first took root in an age when there was a dearth of information, but their role is no less important in an age when there is a glut of the stuff. The process of digesting, simplifying, presenting the relevant and excising the superfluous matters more than ever when more material than anyone could possibly want is pushed onto the Internet every minute. Deciding which bits of the truth are important is what I do every day: it is called editing. Protestants traditionally claim that the Scriptures contain all things necessary for salvation. Broadsheet newspapers claim a sort of secular equivalent: this, they say, is what you need to know in order to be a proper citizen and to avoid looking a fool. Hence slogans like 'No *FT*, no Comment.'

Such large claims as these incline us to abuse our positions. The person who brings a message soon ascertains that his role gives him power. By giving a false message, or an exaggerated one, by withholding a message or by delivering it at great speed, by shouting it when it should be spoken softly or by whispering it when it should be proclaimed from the housetops, he can affect events, advance or retard someone's cause, earn money or lose it, make or break a career. The messenger knows this and, unless he is a saint, he will sometimes exploit this knowledge. No journalist *is* a saint.

There is a gigantic and notorious history of the abuse of press power which I do not propose to rehearse here. I want just to say a little about the most characteristic abuse at the present time. It has something to do with this scrutiny to which everyone in public life is subjected, which I discussed earlier. As the right of scrutiny has grown, so the role of the press has changed. Where once we might have waited, too deferentially, outside a door for a great politician or soldier or prelate to favour us with a few bland words, today we barge in, too arrogantly, to interrogate and arraign. In a world in which to be 'judgemental' is considered very bad we are, in fact, more judgemental than ever. When I was a very young leader writer at the *Daily Telegraph,* my duties seemed chiefly to consist of turning up by 3.45 p.m., writing 400 words about how lazy British workers were and then going home by 7 p.m. And in the succeeding 20 years, the readiness of the media pot to call the kettle black seems to have grown and grown. We are subject to hardly any of the rules of openness, transparency, declarations of interest, accountability, equality of opportunity and conflicts of interest which surround people in public life, and if we were, we could hardly operate at all. Yet we police the most tiny infractions of these rules by others with an unforgiving sternness.

The effect of this is perverse, in at least two ways.

First, in the name of public probity, we set ourselves up as prosecution, judge and jury, without giving the accused the due process of law. In our pursuit of possible iniquity, we regard almost any method of inquiry as legitimate, as we climb over walls and up drainpipes and suborn witnesses in the name of the public's 'right to know'. The *News of the World*'s publication of a list of the whereabouts of sex offenders with spent convictions was a particularly horrifying example. It led to mob violence. I have noticed that many people nowadays have a real terror of the press; even when they have done nothing wrong and have nothing to hide, they have no expectation of being treated fairly or politely. We behave as we do because we claim to speak on behalf of the public interest, but there are plenty of precedents for secret policemen who do what they do 'in the name of the people'. Of course, I am not saying that most of the press is bad most of the time, but there can be little doubt that we have exempted ourselves from the rules we impose upon others. This cannot be good for the immortal souls of journalists, or for telling the truth.

Second, our ferocity in scrutinizing public figures encourages their reluctance to bear witness. This was very apparent in the 2001 election campaign. Almost the main thing that politicians try to do at election-time nowadays is to avoid what lobby journalists call a 'gaffe'. They deliver thousands of words of speech and interview, but they know that 99 per cent of these will pass unnoticed. What they fear is the one sentence or phrase that will get them into trouble. They know that the best minds in journalism will be devoted to catching them out, and they know that virtually no holds are barred. Jeremy Paxman thought it quite appropriate, for example, to ask Mr Hague why nobody liked him, why he wouldn't let his wife speak in public and similar questions which, if asked of one ordinary citizen by another, would earn the questioner a punch on the nose. The conventions of the age meant that Mr Hague had to answer with studious politeness. He was guilty until proved innocent, and so are Mr Blair and Mr Kennedy and all the rest of them. In short, although the media all profess to admire independence of mind, fearlessness and plain speaking; in practice, every politician knows that if he displays these qualities, the media will get him into serious trouble.

My friend and colleague, Boris Johnson, the editor of the *Spectator*, stood as a parliamentary candidate in this election. It was depressing to see journalists writing won-deringly about why on earth he should think of leaving their trade for that of politics – surely no one should have to argue for the good of going into public life. But it was even more depressing to reflect that in a way the journal-ists' bafflement is justified. Although our age is, in formal terms, more democratic than ever before, those who play an active part in that democracy are more despised and more powerless than ever before. We journalists, the bystanders rather than the doers, have the advantage. Boris has more chance of getting a large public audience through the printed page than through the Chamber of the House of Commons.

I noticed that on Sunday 27 May 2001, which was decreed to be World Communications Day and which is an occasion for prayer for those in the media, the first lesson in the Missal was about the martyrdom of Stephen.

It prompted rueful thoughts about the difference between his witness and ours. How, I often wonder, would a daily newspaper like my own have reported the great events of the Gospels? The Nativity, I suspect, would have merited nothing more than a brief story about how overcrowding for the census led to a single mother having to give birth in a stable. Definitely not page one. Even the Passion, much better attested by historical record, would surely have been seen by the *Daily Telegraph* of AD 33 as a story about obscure religious disputes among the Jews leading to a public-order problem for the Roman authorities. I can all too easily imagine writing a leader of gentle rebuke to Pontius Pilate for not cracking down hard enough on the extremists. And our news desk would undoubtedly have treated with extreme scepticism any report that the body of the crucified preacher had risen from the dead. We would have been witnessing what Hollywood rightly called 'the greatest story ever told', and we would have missed it.

'What need have we of further witnesses?' cried those who would drag Jesus off to his crucifixion. As much need as ever, I would say; but our age discourages them from coming forward.

2

GYLES BRANDRETH

Reinventing Childhood

I<small>N AN ARTICLE</small> I <small>WROTE</small> which appeared in the *Sunday Telegraph*, I mentioned in passing that the appearance of one of the young nuns I met at the Tyburn convent reminded me of a delightful character who used to feature in one of my sister's comics when I was a child. She was tall and thin and wore round metal-rimmed spectacles, and she was known as 'Lettice Leaf, the Greenest Girl in the School'. I pointed out, in my piece, that having talked to this charming young sister for an hour or more, I quickly realized that she might be innocent but she was far from naive. And it was thinking about 'innocence without naivety' that led me directly to the theme of 'Reinventing Childhood', which I want to address here.

What are my qualifications for discussing this topic? Well, I have children and I was one. I have also been involved in writing books for children, creating games for children, making television programmes for children, and, for quite a few years now, formerly as Chairman and now as a vice-president, I have been associated with the National Playing Fields Association, the NPFA, the national trust of recreational space, the charity that protects playgrounds and playing fields, and believes that every child deserves a place to play.

Let me start by setting out a few parameters, beginning with time and place. I want to look at how childhood has changed within our lifetime and within our culture.

One hundred and fifty years ago, among the mass of the population, there wasn't a childhood we'd recognize. In this country, infant mortality and child labour were the harsh realities of childhood for millions of children over hundreds of years. And child labour, and infant mortality, and hunger, poverty and disease, are the present harsh realities for millions of children in several parts of the so-called developing world.

I'm not talking about modern Africa or Hogarthian London: I'm talking about childhood today, in the West in general, and in the United Kingdom in particular.

How has it changed in the fifty years since the Queen came to the throne? How has childhood altered in the half-century since I was a toddler?

The short answer is, of course, a great deal.

Today, for example, the principal recreation for all young people is watching television. Not long ago the NPFA conducted a substantial survey of children aged 5 to 16 from 57 schools in England, Wales, Scotland and Northern Ireland, 984 girls, 856 boys, and the survey found what other similar surveys have found and I don't think it will surprise you.[1]

In the United Kingdom boys watch an average of 25 hours and 40 minutes of television a week, girls watch an average of 24 hours and 25 minutes. Forty-five per cent of the girls surveyed also spent an average of 5 hours and 10 minutes playing computer and video games. Sixty-eight per cent of the boys spent an average of 7 hours and 5 minutes on video and computer games. The time spent on video games and surfing the Internet has grown steadily through the nineties and today you'll find surveys suggesting children now spend as much as 15 to 20 hours on video games and the Internet in addition to their television viewing.

Whichever survey you look at, it seems that in 2002, for both sexes, there is not less than three full working days per week simply spent in front of the small screen.

Fifty years ago, of course, there was no Internet, there were no video games, there was very little television, and what television there was was seen by very few. There was radio – and for most children radio was the only form of mass-market entertainment beamed into their homes – and, in case you weren't around or have forgotten, let me remind you what the BBC – the sole provider – aimed to deliver to its young listeners in those days.

I am quoting from an official paper written just after the war by one M. E. Jenkin, Assistant Children's Hour Director. 'Generally speaking,' says M. E. Jenkin, 'we cater most for the ten to fourteen age group, though the claims of the little ones are not forgotten . . . Favourite items: Plays head the list for nearly all ages, though our youngest listeners probably prefer stories . . . S. G. Hulme Beaman's Toytown stories – first favourite in all our broadcast dialogue stories . . .' You remember? 'Oh, Mr Mayor, I'm Larry the Lamb . . .'

Returning to M. E. Jenkin:

If talks are vivid, simple in phraseology and well
delivered, the older children will be interested in a
great variety of subjects. Talks on animals are always
winners, but we have had very successful series on
world affairs, moths and butterflies, and nature lore
generally, travels, stars, stamps, hobbies, etcetera . . .
A Sunday Children's Hour, and religious broadcasts
for children, began early in the War as a result of a
general realisation of the importance of moral and
ethical instruction in the lives of all peoples. We have,
therefore, devoted a regular five minutes at the end
of Wednesday's Children's Hour to a short religious
talk and a Prayer. On Sundays we aim at giving our
best plays to what is probably our largest audience
of the week. Though not by any means always on
religious themes, these plays usually consist of
Biographies of Great Men and Women of the Past.
We have also had plays about famous Biblical charac-
ters, such as Joseph, David, Elijah, Ruth, St Paul, etc.,
and famous Saints like St Francis and St Anselm . . .
While remembering that entertainment is our
function, and that most children listen after a long
school day, it is our aim to give children the best in
music, drama and story, and so train their tastes, and
open doors to spiritual things which might otherwise
remain closed.

Well done, M. E. Jenkin, but it's a world away from *East-Enders*, isn't it?

Because there was only radio, and Saturday morning cinema, within reach of most children fifty years ago, inevitably, in the post-war years, most children filled most of their free time with play, sport and hobbies, ranging from reading to model-making. Play, sport and hobbies are still part of children's lives today, of course, but they don't absorb the amount of time they once did.

In the NPFA survey, the modern child is spending an average of a little over five hours a week on free-play and non-compulsory sports and games.

Interestingly, the nature of unsupervised free-play doesn't seem greatly to have changed. I recommend an enjoyable comparative study of three generations of children's play in an urban environment produced by Hitoshi Shimamura and Chris Snell in the late nineties.[2] They talked to children, parents and grandparents from the Escourt Street district of Hull and found that play, then and now, was centred on the street.

Chasing games, running games, street football, all were apparently popular with all three generations. There had been some changes down the years. Games that had all but disappeared over half a century included British Bulldog, games involving small balls, throwing and catching games, particularly ones involving chanting rhymes, skipping – once a universal activity for girls, now not even mentioned by the contemporary children of Hull. Largely gone too were Hopscotch, What's the time Mr Wolf?, Grandma's Footsteps, In and Out the Dusty Bluebells and fantasy games like Cowboys and Indians. Interestingly, marbles survive. There aren't the variety of marble games played now as once upon a time, but there's still an enthusiasm for chasing marbles along the gutter.

The favourite trick game of the yesteryear – in Hull at least – involved holding an imaginary piece of thread across the road and asking those walking or cycling past to duck under so as not to break it. This game has gone. Its equivalent today, according to the children interviewed, is to set off car alarms by pushing a car or throwing something at it and then, depending on the courage of the young prankster, either running away or waiting until the owner appears and then describing to them a wholly fictional perpetrator.

'Just chatting', either wandering the streets or sitting on a wall, was an activity valued by all three generations and all three generations mentioned the problem of being moved on by unfriendly adults. Intriguingly, chatting was claimed as a predominantly male activity in the old days while today it is overwhelmingly girls who claim it as a favourite recreation. And, of course, the advent of the mobile phone has added a new dimension – and momentum – to the quality and quantity of 'chatting' among young people.

The recent NPFA national survey chimed in with the Hull findings. Favourite free-time activities for boys were:

football (number one with 41 per cent) and chasing and running games (13 per cent); and for girls: chasing and running games (16 per cent), football (8 per cent), netball (6 per cent) and talking and walking with friends (5 per cent).

When it comes to sport, yes, there was more formal school sport, particularly for boys, two generations ago, but I've seen no evidence to suggest that young people's *enthusiasm* for sport has diminished. In the mid-nineties, on behalf of the Sports Council, the Office of Population Censuses and Surveys conducted a survey of over 4,000 young people aged 6 to 16 and concluded that nine out of ten children both enjoy doing sport and think it is important to keep fit.[3]

So, notwithstanding that three-working-days-a-week commitment to the small screen, it seems that young people, when they play today, are playing much as they ever did, their enthusiasm for sports is undiminished and their choice of sporting possibilities has even broadened.

They may not be as fit as once they were – a recent two-year study of Cambridgeshire schoolchildren concluded that the majority of 7- to 11-year-olds do not have the 'standard' level of fitness for their age groups – but children today are fundamentally healthier than they were half a century ago. In simple terms, they suffer from fewer chronic and fatal diseases.

They breathe cleaner air. In 1951 smoke emissions for England and Wales were 2.36 million tonnes. Thanks to the Clean Air legislation of the fifties, within a decade emissions were down to 1.62 million tonnes. The effect on children? Within twenty years of the end of the Second World War, the hours of winter sunshine have increased by 56 per cent.

And today, more children are getting more years of education. In 1944 out of a population of 48 million, 4.5 million were in school. Five and a half decades on, out of a population of 57 million, 9.75 million are in school. When I was a toddler, school and nursery provision for the under-fives was virtually unknown. Today there are around a million day nursery and playgroup places.

You may not believe this, but it could be too that children are safer today than they were a generation ago. According to RoSPA around 250 children under 15 are killed on our roads each year, a number of them because they are playing in streets unsafe for play. But, while traffic has increased dramatically over fifty years, fatalities and accidents involving children have been contained and Britain has one of the best road-safety records in the world.

In the mid-nineties Barnardos published a survey in which they found that nearly 70 per cent of parents felt their neighbourhood was unsafe and half said they never let their children play outside without adult supervision. The parents said their biggest single fear was strangers. Another survey interviewed a thousand adults and found that, for 95 per cent of parents, their greatest fear was the possible abduction of their child by an unknown stranger.

In fact, the risk of a stranger harming a child is extremely small. Home Office research in 1995 concluded: 'First, children are not becoming more vulnerable to homicide, and secondly, the evidence of homicide by strangers on children has been consistently low.' In 1975 the number of youngsters under 16 killed by someone not known to their victim was seven. In 1994 it was four. The average over the past thirty years has been around 6.8.

Healthier, safer, better fed, more indulged – fifty years ago, holidays were fewer, simpler, more local, today international travel for children is commonplace – with more access to sunshine: that's the lot of the modern child. But happier? That's more difficult to quantify. What makes for happiness? It's easier to pinpoint what makes children unhappy. There has been an explosion in single parenthood and divorce in the past fifty years – which may or may not make for happier adults, but all the surveys suggest that children believe themselves to be happier in homes with two parents and without divorce.

The Children in Crisis Campaign mounted by the Relate organization not so long ago was designed to raise more money to train more counsellors because, in Relate's words, divorce is 'having a devastating effect on children and 150,000 will be affected this year'. There are now more than 1.3 million lone parents in Britain, 90 per cent of them female, bringing up 2.1 million children.

So: healthier, safer, better fed, on the whole materially better off; if not necessarily better educated, undeniably in education for a lot longer. Whether happier or not is debatable. Whether more responsible or not is debatable too. Yes, the number of juvenile crimes has been rising, but apparently the number of young criminals may be falling. One report I read suggested that the number of young criminals had fallen by 40 per cent between the 1970s and the 1990s while the number of crimes continued to grow. The culprits are a hard core of persistent and ever-more-active young offenders.

Of course, it could be that the official statistics offer a picture that is rosier than the reality. Recently, Lord Warner, the chairman of the Youth Justice Board, described a growing gang culture that is drawing thousands of children into making crime a 'lifestyle choice'. According to Lord Warner, mugging and bullying are now rampant among the under-15s, although many incidents go unrecorded because most victims are other children. Lord Warner says, 'We now have a culture where intimidation is part of a kid's natural life.' He maintains there are 400 problem estates in Britain, each with gangs of up to sixty children at risk of becoming hardened criminals. Apparently, the government is targeting youth crime on only seventy of these estates.

Lord Warner also warns that while official exclusion statistics show 4,000 children being expelled from school, some 40,000 children are frequently missing from the register and are consequently potential gang recruits.

What Lord Warner has to tell us about the growing drug culture among the young is equally dispiriting. Use of drugs by children simply wasn't an issue fifty years ago. Today, by their own admission, according to a survey of 14,000 children in 89 secondary schools in England, Scotland and Wales, published in 2002, around a third have tried drugs of some sort – and 'binge drinking' is now commonplace among children as young as 13.

And what about sex?

In 1945 it was estimated that 3 per cent of girls and 6 per cent of boys had had sexual intercourse before the age of 17. By 1953 that had gone up to 26 per cent of girls and 38 per cent of boys. Today some estimates claim the figure is up to 75 per cent overall and I read recently that something like one in three of 14- or 15-year-old girls is now on the Pill. Even so, under-age abortions have risen by a fifth in the past ten years. That's why, in some parts of the country, health clinics offer free condoms to children as young as 13 to enable them to have free-and-easy-no-questions-asked access to contraception in the hope of reducing teenage pregnancies and sexually transmitted diseases. I remember, when I was an MP, in my constituency, on just one quite small estate, there were six girls of 13 who were already mothers. Both the quantity and quality of their childhood had been seriously diminished.

I don't know whether you followed the recent family saga of the 15-year-old girl and the 11-year-old father of her baby. He was let off school to attend the birth of his firstborn and there was a newspaper interview with the girl that if it hadn't been so sad would have been hilarious. Solemnly she explained how she would let her young lover go off to play football with his mates once he'd changed the nappies because you've got to let your man have his freedom. We laugh that we may not weep.

So, yes, childhood has changed. In some ways, as we've seen, undoubtedly for the better. In other ways, I think we can agree, definitely for the worse.

So, what's to be done?

When I was an MP I found I only met two types of people: people with problems and people who were right. The people with problems I could manage; I could empathize even when I couldn't be of much help. The people who were *right* were much more of a challenge. I envied their wonderful certainty.

I don't have all the answers. I usually agree with the last person I met. But I have given some thought to the question of childhood – largely because I enjoyed mine and I carry it with me still – and I have a modest manifesto to lay before you.

There are just three planks to it – and three rallying cries.

The first is quite straightforward: every child deserves a place in which to play.

Half a century ago there were more children in rural areas and they played along the lanes and in woods and fields. City children played in playgrounds, yes, and parks, but mainly in the streets and on bomb-sites. Now fewer children live in the country and the opportunities for free-play in the countryside are much reduced. Walking through the long grass, discovering the bluebell wood, crossing streams on stepping stones, clambering up haystacks – as a child I had a chance to do all that as part and parcel of everyday life: today's children don't.

In towns, the bomb-sites have disappeared and the streets are much more heavily trafficked. What's more, in town and country alike, there's now a perception – to which I'll return – that it is more dangerous to wander from home than it used to be. All of which means that when we remodel and develop our communities these days, when we design new streets, new estates, we need to be sure to bear in mind the play and recreation needs of children. It would be inconceivable to build even one house nowadays without provision for car parking, yet you can build an entire estate without providing safe playspace for children. Twenty per cent of the population is under 16: they are the prime users of our streets on foot and bike and they've been woefully neglected down the years.

That we can change – simply by changing the planning regulations to require proper provision for places for young people to play at the heart of the community.

The second: every child deserves some adult attention.

In the past fifty years we've been pretty effective at subcontracting the rearing of the young. Baby-minding subcontracted to the nursery and the crèche; education subcontracted to the schools; discipline to the police; entertainment to the video; feeding to the microwave. With the advent of grazing – eating as and when you want – with the proliferation of in-your-bedroom TVs (two-thirds of children now have their own set in their rooms), we can even avoid having to talk to our children at meal-times.

Lord Warner, chairman of the Youth Justice Board, believes that adults nowadays are not engaged in the lives of children. He says, 'Kids coming out of school are pushing, shoving, talking. The adult world is blind to it. Their mental map is that "this is just kids".'

We mustn't shrug our shoulders or tut-tut from the sidelines. If we want to make a difference, we must get engaged. We must reinvent ourselves as active citizens.

We need sane, normal, balanced, ordinary men and women to get involved in the lives of children. We're not short of people to say all the right things, to conduct research, to produce plans and standards and theses and schemes; we're not short of people with top-down solutions; we're short of people with bottom-up commitment. We're running out of men and women on the ground. We're running out of adults ready, willing and able to give the time, energy, talent and leadership at grass-roots level. They're there, but we need so many more of them.

The truth is, a well-used playing field is hardly ever under threat. A pitch that has kids playing on it week in week out around the year isn't going to be lost to development. But to have a pitch that thrives you need men and women to organize, instruct, referee, motivate, participate, and make it happen.

If you have a small estate populated by listless young teenagers and someone comes along and organizes, say, a theatre group – taking the church hall and putting on a show, then something amazing happens: a creative process with a beginning, a middle and an end, a period of communal activity culminating in a sense of achievement, a chance for everyone to participate – making the sets, designing the posters, playing the music, selling the tickets. It's brilliant, but it only happens if there's an adult to make it happen.

I think we all know, at least in part, how this shortage of people has come about. We, like the young, are spending more time in front of the box. In terms of our recreation and leisure, we're spoilt for choice and pleasurable self-indulgence. There's more competition for our time and we've less time to spare. Our working lives have changed. When my mother married my father 95 per cent of married women were housewives. A generation ago, my father could be a senior partner in a firm of solicitors and stay comfortably on top of his job by working from 9.30 a.m. to 5.30 p.m. He had time to take part in community activities – the local drama group, teaching at Sunday school. Now the ambitious would-be achiever works from 8.30 a.m. to 7 p.m, and when he gets home rightly he's expected to make rather more of a domestic contribution than once upon a time. That's why organizations like the Round Table are facing a crisis over falling membership. The number of children and young people going in for scouting and guiding is as great as it was half a century ago; the problem is finding the leaders.

It may be there's no simple single solution to this dilemma. It may be that we have to accept the philosophy of William Blake that 'He who would do good must do it by minute particulars' and continue to do what we can in small ways: encouraging volunteering, providing sports leadership awards, giving greater recognition and support to those who make a difference on the ground within their communities. Or perhaps we do need what the French call a *grand projet* to jump-start the process? The Duke of Edinburgh Award Scheme is a concept of genius – and one that has been thriving for almost fifty years. Perhaps we need a latter-day Duke of Edinburgh to invent a parallel scheme to recruit and train an army of adults ready to commit themselves to voluntary youth leadership?

And mention of the Duke of Edinburgh leads me, a little circuitously, to the final plank in my manifesto. I am a great admirer of the Duke's, for a variety of reasons. I salute his achievements. I like his style. Every time he makes an apparently politically incorrect remark I want to cheer.

On the whole, like you, I'm not very comfortable with political correctness, but I recognize its power. And it's been thinking about political correctness that has led me to the fundamental answer to the challenge that I am seeking to address here.

Our lives are getting longer, the span has lengthened for both sexes by several years in the past half-century, but over the same period the length of what we would recognize and remember as pure childhood has been reduced by anything from three to five years.

Children are aware of sex, drugs, drink, violence, bad language and cynicism earlier in their lives than ever before.

If this made them happier and healthier children, I might go along with it. If it made them happier and healthier adults, you might even too. But it doesn't. It's come about for a myriad of reasons – it's a reflection of the world in which we now live, where children are sexualized before their time, where television, magazines, advertising, the pop industry and all of us – well, most of us – connive in encouraging a premature pseudo-sophistication that robs children of years of innocence that can never be retrieved.

So what do we do? There are three obvious possibilities:

We shake our heads and sigh and talk nostalgically of the age when there were standards that everybody accepted as the norm.

We pray – and there are several listening to me now who do exactly that.

We hope for a resurgence of faith and cheer on the evangelicals whose style may not be quite to our taste but whose solid achievements have to be recognized.

And there's a fourth. We bring political correctness into play.

Manifest sexism is taboo these days. And quite right too. Fifty years ago it was institutionalized. When I started out on the after-dinner speaking circuit thirty years ago, racist humour was commonplace. Not any more. And quite right too. When it crops up these days, it makes the headlines. Attitudes can change – and for the better.

We need to make it socially unacceptable for anyone – parent, teacher, editor, broadcaster, advertiser and merchandiser – to encroach on the innocence of the young.

It's do-able. To my surprise, I read in the *Independent* recently a piece by a feminist that simply said that the premature sexualization of girls was destroying their childhood.

Essentially, children are exactly the same as they ever were. The phenomenon of Harry Potter proves that. The most successful series of children's books in the history of the world are old-fashioned yarns set in an old-fashioned boarding school wreaking of traditional values and the kind of magic that J. M. Barrie or Enid Blyton would have been proud to have conjured up.

Tyburn was once a place of execution.

The last person to be beheaded in England was one Jeremiah Brandreth. The year was 1817. With others he was accused of insurrection, tried for treason, hanged and then – as an example to others – beheaded with an axe. He was known as the 'The Hopeless Radical'.

Well, I prefer to see myself as 'the hopeful radical'. My radical message is a simple one: let's reinvent childhood. Most of us know the best of it because we've been there. Maybe we can't recapture it as once it was – the blue skies, the bluebell woods, running through long grass, curling up by the fire with the magic of E. Nesbit or the adventures of The Secret Seven. That was fifty years ago. Time passes. Things change. No turning back.

And certainly, even if we could, we wouldn't want to turn the clock back to the harsh reality of childhood for so many a century and more ago.

So let's reinvent childhood for our age, establish it and extend it, and help our children hold onto it – not as something nostalgic or sentimental – but as something contemporary and exciting and real, a time in life when a young person can take innocence and freedom and safety for granted. '**Every child deserves a childhood**'; that's all I want to say.

Notes

1   *Champions – or Couch Potatoes?* NPFA Annual Report, 1990.
2   *They Don't Play Out Like They Used To, Do They?* H. Shima-
    mura and C. Snell, 1996.
3   *The Sports Council's National Survey of Young People and Sport,*
    1994.

3

CHERIE BOOTH

A Catholic Perspective on Human Rights

I am not the evangelizer of democracy, I am the
evangelizer of the Gospel. To the Gospel message,
of course, belongs all the problems of human rights,
and if democracy means human rights
then it also belongs to the message of the Church.

(Pope John Paul II, quoted in Roberto Suro, 'Pope, on Latin Trip,
attacks Pinochet Regime', *New York Times*, 1 April 1987, p. A1 at A10)

Tyburn

The Tyburn lecture is intended as a memorial to the people executed on the gallows known as the Tyburn Tree. Tyburn was the place of execution reserved for crimes directed against the body politic (the King's person/the State), which is to say 'treason'. As such some 50,000 people were put to death here over the 600 or so years that it served as a place of execution from the twelfth century. The form of execution was often the ritual torture of being hanged, drawn and quartered.

That was the fate suffered by the last of the martyrs to die at Tyburn, St Oliver Plunkett. Earlier in the year when we visited the Pope, we stayed in the Pontifical Irish College. It was the Alma Mater of St Oliver and where he signed the oath promising to return to Ireland after ordination. Seeing that oath was a vivid reminder of the price paid by earlier generations for our contemporary religious, social and political liberty.

As Elizabeth I consolidated her father's break with Rome, continued allegiance to the Pope was regarded in England as an act of treason. The Monarch claimed to be able to exercise full imperial powers within his own realm – *Rex est in regno suo imperator* – which meant that he was subordinate and subject to no-one but God. This high theory of imperial kingship carried with it a right to govern the Church. One result of this redefinition/realignment of the English body politic was that from 1531 up to

1681 some 105 people were executed for their Catholic faith. Of course throughout the Middle Ages there were frequent tensions between monarchs and popes. This came more sharply into focus at the time of the Reformation.

We see, then, in Tyburn a place where the State claimed the authority of life and death over all those finding themselves within its territorial jurisdiction. And in its execution of Catholic martyrs, it was clearly also a State which claimed the right to bind the consciences of individuals in religious matters and to impose a degree of uniformity in religious practice and allegiance. A State, in other words, which denied individuals' fundamental rights – namely the right to life and the right to freedom of conscience, to religious liberty and toleration.

Tyburn then is a monument, a memorial to the idolatrous State which sees itself as the regulator of people's consciences and reserved to itself the power of life and death. A State which did not then respect the injunction of rendering unto 'Caesar that which is Caesar's and to God that which is God's'. It was instead an absolutist State which arrogated to itself powers which did not belong to it and falsely claimed a divine right to its kingship or dominion. In our society Catholics were at the receiving end, while in other parts of Europe roles were reversed.

Today, our country is a pluralist society of faiths and a very different environment to the one our forefathers experienced at Tyburn. Catholics and people of other faiths are integrated into society in a way unimaginable only one hundred years ago. Intra-faith is taken for granted – inter-faith is the new challenge.

It seems highly appropriate then that in a lecture memorializing this place of execution and of martyrdom, we should be talking about human rights. Because human rights are precisely about setting limits on state power: affirming that there are properly limits in law and morality beyond which the State cannot trespass; that there is a sphere of individual personal autonomy which the State must respect and, indeed, provide the conditions within which individuals may flourish as individuals.

Catholicism and human rights

There is no doubt that the language of human rights, when it first emerged in the throes of the French Revolution and the Enlightenment attack on religion, was viewed by the Church with suspicion. It was seen as part of a secularist project, aimed at removing religion and religious practice from the body politic. Thus it was thought to be a continuation of an attack by the State on the Church. If the Reformation was seen from a Catholic perspective as subordinating the Church to the State, the Enlightenment was seen as an attempt by the State to completely remove the Church from public life.

But the Church's suspicions over the language of human rights have long since gone and today one of the foremost exponents of human rights is the present pope.[1] Pope John Paul II has said many times that human rights are at the centre of the Church's concerns.

And in his address in October 1995 to the Fiftieth General Assembly of the United Nations Organization, Pope John Paul emphasized the natural law and fundamental moral status of human rights when he observed as follows:

> It is a matter for serious concern that some people today deny the universality of human rights, just as they deny that there is a human nature shared by everyone. To be sure, there is no single model for organizing the politics and economics of human freedom; different cultures and different historical experiences give rise to different institutional forms of public life in a free and responsible society. But it is one thing to affirm a legitimate plurality of 'forms of freedom' and another to deny any universality or intelligibility to the nature of man or to the human experience.

It is significant that it is the development of human rights after World War II that has received the specific endorsement of the Church. The Pope recognizes that we live in a 'post-Nuremberg Europe', that is to say, a Europe ineradicably marked and changed by the experience of the perversion of law and the utter tyranny of State power which characterized the years of Nazi rule in Germany and occupied Europe from the early 1930s to the mid-1940s. This is no coincidence. It must always be remembered that Pope John Paul II lived as a young man under the tyranny of Nazi-occupied Poland. As President Bush said in Krakow in May 2003: 'Karol Wojtyla saw the swastika flag flying over the ramparts of Wawel Castle. He shared the suffering of his people and was put into forced labour. From this priest's experience and faith came a vision: that every person must be treated with dignity, because every person is known and loved by God.'

The Nazi State: law without rights

The unique horror of the Nazi system is that it purported to maintain the forms of law and legality, while permitting tyranny and injustice to reign. Under the Nazi State, however, the legal system not only provided for punishment and death, it allowed for torture to be used against individuals. It routinely reversed the presumption of innocence and the principle that criminal legislation should not be applied retrospectively. It legislated for people to be held in slavery and conditions of forced labour. It grossly interfered in the rights to privacy of those under its rule, and denied them rights to free expression, free assembly and to freedom of thought, conscience and religion. The Nazi authorities in the name of 'eugenics' withdrew from certain individuals the right to marry and to found a family. Notoriously, they discriminated amongst the populations under their control on the grounds of race, religion, sexual orientation, national and social origin and political or other opinion. In the words of the Nuremberg War Crimes Tribunal, the Nazi legal system was one which nurtured:

> a nation-wide government-organized system of cruelty and injustice, in violation of the laws of war and of humanity, and perpetrated in the name of law by the authority of the Ministry of Justice and through the instrumentality of the courts. The dagger of the assassin was concealed beneath the robe of the jurist.

All the while, however, the German legal system continued to function in other ways, with the courts resolving disputes among those of appropriate Aryan ancestry over questions of succession to estates, claims for divorce and custody, matters of contract, employment rights and jurisdiction. The grotesque nature of such a legal system lies in the fact that all the rules which it sets out, no matter their content, continued to be applied according to the classic methods of legal reasoning. Judges and lawyers considered the text of the laws passed by the governing authorities and attempted to apply those laws to the factual situations presented before them. The forms of rationality and objectivity were maintained, but the substance of the law was surrendered to sheer barbarism. The law become a mere idol, in the sense that the Psalmist uses it (Psalms 115.5–6), as having a mouth that did not speak, eyes that did not see, ears that did not hear – that is to say a legal system dumb, blind and deaf before the claims of justice.

The 'pre-Nuremberg' response of the lawyer and judge to a claim that the substance of a particular law was unjust or immoral was to say that it was not for them to strike down or refuse to apply a law simply because it was immoral. The lawyer or judge had instead to find a way within the system which rendered the unjust law unlawful – because, for example, it was unconstitutional or it contravened some other provision of positive law. Where, however, the whole legal system had been corrupted, because it legitimized discrimination and, ultimately, the expropriation and extermination of the Jews, then it was not possible for a conscientious judge or lawyer within that system to find to any legal norms to nullify or mitigate the effects of its unequivocally unjust laws. The pre-Nuremberg response, then, was wholly inadequate because it permitted evil to operate under the cloak of legitimacy and co-opted lawyers and judges into its actions. It also allowed individuals to disown any moral responsibility for their grossly immoral actions on the ground that they were only carrying out lawful orders and commands.

The Nuremberg War Crime trials were set up in response to this catastrophic failure of the German legal system to keep true to the norms of justice and morality in the face of the idolatry of the State that characterized Nazism. In *United States* v. *Altstötter and others* a selection of some 16 jurists (public prosecutors, presiding judges and officials, lawyers and ministers in the Ministry of Justice) who had assisted in the administration of the legal system during the Nazi era were put on trial for their involvement in 'judicial murder and other atrocities which they committed by destroying law and justice in Germany and by utilizing the empty forms of legal process for persecution, enslavement and extermination on a vast scale'.

The end result of the Nuremberg war-crime trials was the articulation of a new legal order under which individuals were bound by the general principles of international humanitarian law and morality recognized by civilized nations, no matter the terms of their national legal systems. It was no longer an excuse or a defence to a criminal prosecution to say that one was only following orders or applying the law as set down by the governing authorities of the State. Instead (civil) disobedience to the claims of the governing authorities was made into a duty. It is on the basis of this new legal order that war-crimes trials have since been instituted into the genocides in, for example, the former Yugoslavia and Rwanda.

The post-Nuremberg vision: fundamental rights setting limits on the law on state power

But it was not simply in the realms of international law that Nuremberg had an impact. The response to the horrors and excesses of the Nazi State and legal system was also for jurists to come together to set out, both in international charters and national constitutions, the actual substance of the moral underpinnings to the domestic law of states. Thus, the United Nations proclaimed the Universal Declaration of Human Rights in 1948. International regional agreements were also entered into, notably the 1950 European Convention on Human Rights. The post-war German national constitution set out a list of basic rights which the German state was henceforth bound to accept and which could not be changed or abrogated by any constitutional amendment. In the post-war process of decolonization, too, states newly independent of the British Empire were given written constitutions containing bills of fundamental rights modelled on the European Convention.[2] And in the years after the war, Canada, New Zealand and South Africa created and incorporated their own bills or charters of fundamental rights and freedoms. As Lord Bingham has noted:

> Before the Second World War there were no international agreements governing the protection of human rights, which was indeed an expression rarely

used. Gradually and erratically, as very well described by Professor Brian Simpson in *Human Rights and the End of Empire* (2001), chs 4 and 5, such protection emerged as an allied war aim. The Universal Declaration of Human Rights 1948 (which contained nothing equivalent to the reasonable time requirement) was one product of that movement; the European Convention for the Protection of Human Rights and Fundamental Freedoms was a later and much more potent product. Those who negotiated and first signed the Convention were not seeking to provide a blueprint for the ideal society. They were formulating a statement of very basic rights and freedoms which, it was believed, were very largely observed by the contracting states and which it was desired to preserve and protect both in the light of recent experience and in view of developments in Eastern Europe. The Convention was seen more as a statement of good existing practice than as an instrument setting targets or standards which contracting states were to strive to achieve.[3]

On 2 October 2000, the Human Rights Act 1998 came into force here in the UK. The declared intention of the government in bringing forward the Bill was to 'bring rights home'. The Human Rights Act is not a bill of rights in the sense traditionally understood by the term, nor does it confer new rights upon British citizens. Rather, what the

Act does for the first time is to incorporate the rights of the European Convention on Human Rights into domestic law. It should be appreciated that British citizens have held these rights for over half a century – since the UK ratified the Convention in 1951 – and indeed it is an often-noted irony that British lawyers were instrumental in the creation of the Convention, lobbying for its existence and drafting many of its articles. Britain, furthermore, was also one of the first countries to sign up to the Convention. All the more surprising then, that it has taken almost 50 years for its provisions to become part of substantive UK law.

One of the lesser known provisions of the Act is section 13 which provides that if a court's determination of any question arising under the Act might affect the exercise by a religious organization (itself or its members collectively) of the right under Article 9 of the Convention of freedom of thought, conscience and religion, it must have particular regard to the importance of that right. This reinforces the fact that for the first time in English law the Human Rights Act gives explicit support to the freedom of religion. And the liberal assumptions that underpin the Act absolutely allow for and support the practice of religious faith within the law. This recognition by the law of the importance of religious belief is also seen in the new UK Regulations which, with effect from December 2003, will outlaw discrimination in employment on grounds of religion or belief – a development which was prefigured in Northern Ireland's fair employment legislation but which now applies through the whole of the UK (and indeed of the European Union, given that these regulations implement an EU directive).

Since World War II, more and more nations in the world have experienced significant constitutional change or development whether through the creation of the European Union, the dismantling of Communism, the process of decolonization, the transformation of Empire into Commonwealth, or the ending of apartheid. Part of that constitutional change included the incorporation into the structures of the states the insights gained from the post-Nuremberg experience, in particular the need to protect individuals' fundamental rights and set substantive limits on the powers of the State. This embracing and incorporation of fundamental rights standards within national legal systems post-Nuremberg may be seen as a memorial for or legal monument to the victims of Nazism.

Should the State have powers of life and death over individuals?

Although the result of certain of the Nuremberg war-crime trials was that sentence of death was pronounced against a number of individuals indicted before it, one of the developing post-war insights into the requirements for the proper protection of fundamental rights is that the death penalty is unacceptable. For example, the Sixth Protocol to the European Convention, dating from 1983, provides that: 'The death penalty shall be abolished. No-one shall be condemned to such penalty or executed.' This is a right that has been incorporated into UK law by the Human Rights Act 1998. And there has been a growing amount of case law – under the European Convention, the South African Constitution and the Canadian Charter of Rights – to the effect that to expose an individual to the possibility of the death penalty violates their rights to fundamental justice and/or the right not to be subjected to cruel, inhuman or degrading punishment. This developing jurisprudence against capital punishment might also be understood as the legacy of Nuremberg and the memory of the excesses of fascism.

In his 1995 encyclical *Evangelium vitae* Pope John Paul concluded that in most cases there was no longer any moral basis to justify the use of the death penalty by the State. Yet on 25 January 2002, Justice Antonin Scalia, one of the nine judges who make up the bench of the Supreme Court of the United States – and one of the three Catholics on that bench – addressed a conference held at the University of Chicago on the topic 'Religion, Politics and the Death Penalty'. Justice Scalia made clear, at the outset, that his remarks had nothing to do with how he might vote as a judge in any particular case. He also stated that he took no public position on the policy desirability, or otherwise, of capital punishment. What he was concerned with was whether or not it could properly be said that the authorities of the State had no moral right ever to impose and execute the death penalty. His concern with this moral question came from the fact that, as a judge within a legal system which does allow for capital punishment, his vote in any death-penalty case before the US Supreme Court could determine whether or not the authorities would go ahead and put an individual to death. He concluded therefore that:

> the choice for the judge who believes the death penalty to be immoral is resignation rather than simply ignoring duly enacted constitutional laws and sabotaging the death penalty. He has, after all, taken an oath to apply those laws, and has been given no power to supplant them with rules of his own.

Justice Scalia then set out his personal view that the State had a moral right to impose the death penalty and that he saw no justification for civil disobedience in the sense that an individual citizen might be justified in disobeying an unjust law. He concluded his address with a reaffirmation of the proper limits of the judicial role. He remained publicly neutral on the policy question as to whether there ought to be capital punishment. His view was, simply: that the State was not prevented by moral considerations from maintaining the death penalty, and that those who participated in the State's lawful imposition of the sentence of death were not co-operating in an evil act. He warned that if the 'Church's new, albeit non-binding position' on the immorality of the death penalty were imposed on the faithful, then this would require American Catholics to withdraw from public life because it would effectively disqualify them from running for political office, from sitting as judges, from working as criminal prosecutors, or from serving on juries. This was not, he suggested, the course of prudence.

Even though we no longer have the death penalty in the UK, there will be circumstances when our judges too have to wrestle with the same moral, legal and constitutional dilemmas placed upon the Justices of the Supreme Court of the United States. Does this mean that they too would be forced to resign over matters of conscience?

As was pointed out in a *Tablet* article from 2002 by my Matrix colleague Aiden O'Neill QC[4] Justice Scalia was right, at least, to point out that for individuals to be able to participate properly and conscientiously within the legal system (whether as a judge, lawyer or juror) there has to be a congruence between what their legal duties are, and what they see to be their moral duties. But his assertion that those who oppose the death penalty as immoral can there-fore no longer participate as officials within the legal system is more problematic. This claim might only be jus-tified if Justice Scalia was correct in his legal judgment that US law *obliged* judges to implement the death penalty.

Laws in the United States, however enacted, have to be in accordance with the requirements of the US Constitu-tion and its Bill of Rights. Constitutional Amendment VIII of 1791 provides that 'Excessive bail shall not be required, nor excessive fines imposed, nor cruel and unusual punishment inflicted.' Justice Scalia's view is that the question of what is cruel and unusual punishment has to be judged by the standards of the founders of the Constitution and not of the present day.

There is, however, another interpretation that can be made of the Constitution which would give those working within the US legal system who accept recent papal teaching on the death penalty a choice other than resignation from their posts. Such jurists may, instead, reject Scalia's strict constructionism and choose to interpret the US Constitution as a 'living instrument', in the way we in Europe interpret the European Convention on Human Rights. In accordance with *Evangelium vitae*, the moral principle of respect for life, combined with consideration of the existing constitutional prohibition against the infliction of cruel and unusual punishment, may lead US lawyers to a proper **legal** judgment that the infliction of the death penalty is not only immoral, but is also unconstitutional and so unlawful. The Pope's encyclical, then, does not require the mass resignation of Catholics from public legal life. It just requires them to inform their interpretation of the US Constitution with the legal and moral insights gained after Nuremberg, namely that the law must always show respect for the life of every individual, no matter their race, their religion or, indeed, their crime. Constitutional law of all law should be able to learn the lessons of history and adapt and change as society progresses.

Human rights within the Catholic Church?

As Justice Scalia's concerns make clear, the Church has been at the forefront of this renewed emphasis on the moral and legal limits on the competences and powers of the State and its particular duty to respect the dignity of each individual. The Church has also endorsed the notion that the rightly ordered State had strictly limited and legally defined powers, primarily to do with the protection of individuals' fundamental rights and the maintenance of the public order necessary for civil society's pursuit of the common good.

In 1967, the Synod of Bishops on 'Justice in the World' declared:

> While the Church is bound to give witness to justice, it recognizes that everyone who ventures to speak to people about justice must first be just in their eyes. Hence we must undertake an examination of the modes of acting and of the possessions and lifestyle found within the Church herself.

Thus the present Pope has explicitly acknowledged that the Church's own historical human-rights record has been less than perfect. He has therefore taken the unprecedented step of acknowledging the Church's own institutional guilt and has apologized to various groups in whose persecution the institutional Church was complicit, notably the persecution of Jews under the Inquisition. The Church has prided itself on being at the forefront of the fostering and the practical defence of women's rights, most notably the right of women to education and to health care, particularly in the developing world and fundamentalist societies where all too often being a woman means being condemned to a life of poverty, ignorance and disease. The Church has exhorted the international community to 'strive to help women to live their full dignity by exercising those political, economic, social and cultural rights which have been recognized in the Universal Declaration of Human Rights'.[5]

The Church rightly sees it as its duty to speak on human rights internationally where they have considerable influence but no direct power to effect change. What about the question of respect for human rights within the Church itself, in areas where the Church has not only moral authority, but also actual authority to make a difference? One thinks for example of the need for fair procedures, for what used to be called natural justice; this is as important for the priest under scrutiny – and perhaps suspicion of serious wrongdoing – as it is for any other citizen in society. Scripture itself gives us a radical message of the fundamental equality before God of all in the Church, as

St Paul says in the Letter to the Galatians (3.28): '[In] Christ there are no more distinctions between Jew and Greek, slave and free, male and female,[6] but all of you are one in Christ Jesus.'

This vision of equality before God and under the law is reflected also in the Second Vatican Council's 1964 Pastoral Constitution on the Church in the Modern World (*Gaudium et spes*) where it is stated in Article 29(2), in language consciously echoing both Article 2 of the 1948 Universal Declaration of Human Rights[7] and Article 14 of the European Convention on Human Rights[8] that: 'Any kind of social or cultural discrimination in basic personal rights on the grounds of sex, race, colour, social conditions, language or religion must be curbed and eradicated as incompatible with God's design.'

The Church is a pilgrim Church. It has not yet arrived at its destination. It is not perfect. It may be that the implications of the radical equality proclaimed in Galatians and Vatican II (and now set forth in the civil law of the European Convention on Human Rights) will in time come to change perceptions on the role of women within the Church. Certainly in my lifetime there has been a sea change in the visibility of women in the Church. In my pre-Vatican II childhood, women were seen but not heard in the Church. The Second Vatican Council changed all that. In the Council Fathers' closing message they said:

The hour is coming, in fact has come, when the vocation of women is being acknowledged in its fullness, the hour in which women acquire in the world, an influence, an effect and a power never hitherto achieved. That is why, at this moment when the human race is undergoing so deep a transformation, women imbued with a spirit of the gospel can do so much to aid humanity in not falling.

Pope John Paul has laid out a new perspective on the role of women in the Church in his 1988 Apostolic Letter *Mulieris dignitatem*. The Church has still some way to go in practically introducing his concepts into church and lay life, but as in many other areas, he is often ahead of his time. In particular, the Pope speaks of the 'feminine genius' and that the Christian Gospel is in 'consistent protest with whatever offends the dignity of women'. The concept of the 'feminine genius' will have varying interpretations and, as I have indicated, historically the Church has not always lived up to that interpretation of the Gospel. But today and in the future we must work towards realizing this vision of an integral role for women, and indeed for the laity, in the Church; demographical changes alone make this essential.

In England and Wales today, and in the Church worldwide, we see that spirit moving and the laity playing a far more public role in the Church. Indeed there are often more lay people in the sanctuary than there are clergy as lay people take up their roles as Eucharistic ministers, readers, cantors and servers. Laity are now more engaged at both parish and diocesan level. In some dioceses we are already seeing some green shoots with the appointment of female religious chancellors, etc. Canon law seems to be following civil law in opening its doors to greater female participation. A generation ago there were few if any female canon lawyers, but now that is changing and as the pool expands we can expect to see many more female and lay judges working in the ecclesiastical courts.

In the sacramental life of the Church, canon law expressly recognizes that where ministers are not available lay people can exercise the ministry of the word, preside over liturgical prayers, confer baptism and distribute Holy Communion.[9] All this is rightly encouraged by the Church's hierarchy. But there is still a sense in which some in the Church see women as the 'praying Church' and the 'working Church' but not the 'thinking Church'; they are embraced as handmaidens but not as thinkers or leaders. Women are still seen as progressing the ideas of the masculine other in the Church rather than being acknowledged for what the 'feminine genius' can contribute in its own right to the Church. On my recent visit to the Vatican, for example, I thought that there could be greater scope for active female participation in the Curia.

Some in the Church's hierarchy and especially in our own country are responding to these trends. I welcome the recent homily by Archbishop Puente, the Papal Nuncio at the European Conference of the World Union of Catholic

Women's organizations.[10] He called upon Catholic women to be true to their mission in speaking out about the role of women in society and in the Church today and to take up the challenge which Christ gave to Mary Magdalene when he met her in the Garden on Easter Sunday. He said to Mary: 'Go and find my brothers and tell them: I am ascending to my Father and your Father.' In so doing he appointed her his witness and the messenger of the Resurrection to the apostles.[11]

In May 2003, I hosted a reception at No. 10 for the Margaret Beaufort Institute of Theology in Cambridge, which prepares women for service in the mission of the Church. I was minded of what Cardinal Cormac Murphy-O'Connor said at the Institute last year. He said: 'the time has come, belatedly, for the role of women in the Church as co-workers in collaborative ministry to become a reality. Not a subject of conjecture, but a goal to be achieved.'

There is still more that we can do, not least at the parish, diocesan, national and international structures of the Church, to be more inclusive. The renewal of the Church demands that each of us play a part. The hierarchy has an obligation to 'acknowledge and foster the ministries, the offices and the role of the lay faithful'.[12] Meaningful space must be created in which service can thrive and grow. Lay people need to develop a more generous and willing spirit and to be prepared to step forward and serve. It is incumbent on us all to realize the doctrine of the 'priesthood of all believers' which was so strongly reaffirmed at the

Second Vatican Council. Further realization of that doctrine can be a faithful calling, a real challenge and a tremendous vehicle of renewal in the Church and the world.

Notes

1 See, too, the English Catholic Bishops' 1998 Booklet *Human Rights and the Catholic Church* which was sent to parishes across England and Wales.

2 See Professor Brian Simpson, *Human Rights and the End of Empire* (Oxford, 2001). See, too, *Reyes* v. *The Queen* [2002] 2 AC 235, JCPC per Lord Bingham refers to it in at 245 paragraph 23:

> [An] important development has been the advance to independent statehood of many former colonies under entrenched Constitutions expressed to be the supreme law of the state. In the majority of such countries, as in Belize, the practice was adopted of setting out in the Constitution a series of fundamental rights and freedoms which were to be protected under the Constitution. It is well-established that in drafting the chapters containing these statements of rights heavy reliance was placed on the European Convention, first in drafting the Constitution of Nigeria and then in drafting those of Jamaica and many other states around the world: see *Minister of Home Affairs* v. *Fisher* [1980] AC 319, 328, Simpson, *Human Rights and the End of Empire* (Oxford, 2001), pp. 863–72 and Demerieux, *Fundamental Rights in Commonwealth Caribbean Constitutions* (University of West Indies, 1992), p. 23.

3 *Dyer* v. *Watson* [2002] 1 WLR 1388, JCPC per Lord Bingham at 1506–7.

4 'Choose life not death', 23 February 2002.

5 See Dr Suzanne Scorsone, *Statement on Behalf of the Holy See to the 42nd Session of the UN Commission on the Status of Women*, delivered on 3 March 1998 and reported in *L'Osservatore Romano*, Weekly Edition in English, v31, n17(1539), 29 April 1998.

6 In David Lodge's *How Far Can You Go* (Penguin), a character adds 'gay or straight' to this list, but that may be going too far (for St Paul at least).

7 Article 2(1) of the Universal Declaration of Human Rights provides that:

> Everyone is entitled to all the rights and freedoms set forth in this Declaration without distinction of any kind, such as race, colour, sex language, religion, political or other opinion, national or social origin, property, birth or other status.

8 Article 14 of the European Convention on Human Rights provides that:

> The enjoyment of the rights and freedoms set forth in this Convention shall be secured without discrimination on any grounds such as sex, race, colour, language, religion, political or other opinion, national or social origin, association with a national minority, property, birth or other status.

9 Can. 230.3.

10 18 March 2003.

11 John 20.17.

12 *Christi fideles laici* No. 33.

4

GEORGE WEIGEL

The Free and Virtuous Society

Catholic Social Doctrine in the Twenty-First Century

CHRISTIANS HAVE BEEN THINKING THROUGH their relationship to the tangled worlds-within-worlds of politics, economics and culture for nearly two millennia. The essential nature of that unavoidable entanglement and the distinctive character of the Christian's presence in 'the world' came into focus early. As the *Letter to Diogne-tus*, most likely written in the second century, reminds us, Christians are always 'resident aliens' in the world, for while Christians honour just rulers, obey just laws, and contribute to the common good of whatever society in which they find themselves, a Christian's ultimate loyalty is given to a kingdom that is elsewhere. Christians believe that history can only be read in its fullness in the light of faith in the Risen Christ, the Lord of history. And in that perspective, history is both the arena of God's action and the antechamber to our true home, the 'city of the living God' (Heb. 12.22). Those who know *that* about history live in history in a distinctive way.[1]

One might think that this two-edged conviction about the present and the future absolves Christians from responsibility for politics, economics and culture, and some Christians have in fact regarded a quietistic with-drawal from the world and its affairs as a demand of discipleship. Catholic faith takes a different stance, however. The Catholic Church believes that it is precisely because Christians live their lives 'in the world' by refer-ence to transcendent truth and love that Christians can offer their neighbours a word of genuine hope amidst the flux of history. Because Christians live both *in* time and *ahead of* time – because Christians are the people who know how the human story turns out, viz., in the final vindication of God's salvific purposes – Christians are in a unique position vis-à-vis history, politics, economics and culture. As Hans Urs von Balthasar has put it, amidst the world's accelerating development Christians are the people who 'can confront [that development] with a divine plan of salvation that is co-extensive with it, that indeed always runs ahead of it because it is eschatological'.[2]

Over the centuries, there have been numerous Christian proposals for understanding the Church's relationship to the world of politics, economics and culture; H. Richard Niebuhr's classic, *Christ and Culture*, still offers a useful typology of the five principal approaches.[3] Surely one of the most intellectually important Christian efforts to shed the light of the Gospel on public life has been the tradition of Catholic social doctrine. Reaching back to the classical and medieval masters for its inspiration while putting their insights into conversation with the realities of the contemporary world, modern Catholic social doctrine has always had a distinctive *public* quality to it, beginning with Leo XIII's pioneering 1891 encyclical, *Rerum novarum*. Unlike certain other Christian explications of the Church's position in the world, which speak essentially to the believing community, Catholic social doctrine has been thoroughly ecumenical in the full sense of the *oikumene*: Catholic social doctrine has understood itself as being 'not for Catholics only'. Although the phrase does not appear until John XXIII, the social doctrine of the Church has always been addressed to 'all men and women of good will'. It is a genuinely *public* proposal, using analyses and arguments about public goods and the means to achieve them that can be engaged by any intelligent person.

From the years prior to Pope Leo's writing *Rerum novarum* to the present, Catholic social doctrine has evolved in a collaborative dialogue between the successors of Peter and theologians. I would like to suggest where that dialogue and that papal teaching have led us in this first decade of a new century and a new millennium, so that we can better understand the areas where Catholic social doctrine requires development in the years immediately ahead.

The contribution of John Paul II

The social magisterium of John Paul II assumes, even as it develops, the three great principles that have shaped the Church's social doctrine since Leo XIII; John Paul has also cemented a fourth principle into the foundations of Catholic social doctrine.

The first classic principle is the *principle of personalism*, which can also be called the *human-rights principle*. According to this foundation stone of the Church's social doctrine, all right thinking about society – in its cultural, political and economic aspects – begins with the inalienable dignity and value of the human person. Right thinking about society does not begin, in other words, with the State, the party, the tribe, the ethnic group or the gender group. It begins with the individual human person. Society and its legal expression, the State, must always be understood to be in service to the integral development of the human person. The State, in particular, has an obligation to defend the basic human rights of persons, which are 'built into' us by reason of our very humanity. 'Rights', in the Catholic understanding of the term, are not benefices distributed by the State at its whim or pleasure; they are goods to be protected and/or advanced by any just state.

The second classic principle is the *principle of the common good*, or what we can call the *communitarian principle*; it complements and completes the personalist principle. Because men and women grow into the fullness of their humanity through relationships, each of us should exercise our rights in such a way that that exercise contributes to the general welfare of society, and not simply to our individual aggrandizement. Living in service to the common good is essential for the integral development of persons as well as for the good of society.

The third classic principle is the *principle of subsidiarity*, which we can call the *free-associational principle* or *principle of civil society*. It was first given magisterial form in Pius XI's 1931 encyclical, *Quadragesimo anno*, although its vision of a richly textured and multi-layered human society reaches back to medieval Christian experience. The principle of subsidiarity teaches us that decision-making in society should be left at the lowest possible level (i.e., the level closest to those most effected by the decision), commensurate with the common good. American 'federalism' is one empirical example of the principle of subsidiarity at work. Articulated under the lengthening shadow of the totalitarian project in the first third of the twentieth century, the principle of subsidiarity remains today as a counter-statist principle in Catholic social thinking. It directs us to look first to private-sector solutions, or to a private-sector/public-sector mix of solutions, rather than to the State, in dealing with urgent social issues such as education, health care and social welfare.[4]

These were the foundational principles inherited by John Paul II, principles he taught in his pre-episcopal days as a seminary lecturer on social ethics. As Pope, John Paul has added a fourth principle to the foundations of the Church's social doctrine: the *principle of solidarity*, or what we can call the *principle of civic friendship*. A society fit for human beings, a society capable of fostering integral human development, cannot be merely contractual and legal, John Paul teaches; it needs a more richly textured set of relationships. It requires what Jacques Maritain used to describe as 'civic friendship': an experience of fellow-feeling, of brotherhood, of mutual participation in a great common enterprise. A genuinely human society flourishes when individuals dedicate the exercise of their freedom to the defence of others' rights and the pursuit of the common good, and when the community supports individuals as they grow into a truly mature humanity – that is what living 'in solidarity' means.[5] Here, we note, is one important way in which the social doctrine of the Church is clearly distinguished from that prominent current of modern political thought that reduces all social relationships to the contractual. (Americans instinctively understood the false picture of democratic society proposed by a merely contractual understanding of society on September 11, 2001, when great acts of heroism and compassion were done by people who clearly knew that their relationship to their fellow Americans, and to America, was not reducible to the terms of a contract.)

On this four-principled foundation, John Paul II has developed the social doctrine of the Church in five of his encyclicals. Three of these are 'social encyclicals' *stricte dictu*; two other encyclicals address grave questions at the heart of today's 'social question'. Let me highlight here the original contributions of John Paul II to Catholic social doctrine.

In his first social encyclical, *Laborem exercens* (1981), John Paul offered the Church and the world a rich phenomenology of work. Challenging the view that work is a 'punishment' for original sin, the Pope taught that work is both an expression of human creativity and a participation in the sustaining creative power of God.[6] Work is less to be understood as constraint, and more to be understood as an expression of our freedom. Through our work, John Paul urges, we do not simply *make* more; we *become* more.[7] Thus work has a spiritual dimension, and when we identify our work and its hardships with the work, the passion and the death of Christ, our work participates in the development of the Kingdom of God.[8]

In his second social encyclical, *Sollicitudo rei socialis* (1988), John Paul defined, for the first time in Catholic social doctrine, a 'right of economic initiative', which he described as an expression of the creativity of the human person.[9] At a macro-level, the Pope insisted that civil society and its network of free and voluntary associations is essential to economic and political development; the Pope also taught that development economics and economic-development strategies cannot be abstracted from questions of culture and politics. Nor can the problems of underdevelopment be understood, in Catholic perspective, as a question of victimization only; integral human development, John Paul wrote, requires Third World countries to undertake rigorous legal and political reforms. Participatory government, the Pope suggested, is crucial to integral development.[10]

In what seems, in retrospect, a prophetic anticipation of the communist crack-up, John Paul II warned in *Sollicitudo rei socialis* against the dangers to integral human development (at both the individual and societal levels) of a 'blind submission to pure consumerism', a theme to which he would return frequently in the next decade.[11] In another anticipation of the post-Cold War debate, *Sollicitudo rei socialis* also urged the developed world not to fall into 'selfish isolation'; 'interdependence' (a phenomenon that would subsequently evolve into 'globalization') has a moral, not merely material, character, the Pope taught. No country or region can ever be read out of history or simply abandoned.[12]

John Paul II's most developed social encyclical, *Centesimus annus*, was published in 1991 to mark the centenary of *Rerum novarum* and to launch the Church's social doctrine into a new century and millennium. Among its principal themes were the following:

(1) What the Church proposes to the world of the twenty-first century is the *free and virtuous society*. The two are inseparable. The contemporary human quest for freedom is undeniable. But it will be frustrated, and new forms of tyranny will emerge, unless the free society is also a virtuous society.[13]

(2) The free and virtuous society is composed of three interlocking parts – a democratic political community, a free economy and a robust public moral culture. The key to the entire edifice is the cultural sector. Because free politics and free economics let loose tremendous human energies, a vibrant public moral culture is necessary to discipline and direct those energies so that they serve the ends of genuine human flourishing.[14]

(3) Democracy and the free economy are not machines that can run by themselves. It takes a certain kind of people, possessed of certain virtues, to run self-governing polities and free economies so that they do not self-destruct. The task of the moral-cultural sector is to form these habits of heart and mind in people, and the primary public task of the Church is to form that moral-cultural sector. Thus the Church is not in the business of proposing technical solutions to questions of governance or economic activity; the Church is in the business of forming the culture that can form the kind of people who can develop those solutions against a transcendent moral horizon.[15]

(4) Freedom must be tethered to moral truth and ordered to human goodness if freedom is not to become self-cannibalizing.[16]

(5) Voluntary associations – the family, business associations, labour unions, social and cultural groups – are essential to the free and virtuous society. They embody what John Paul calls the 'subjectivity of society', and they are crucial schools of freedom.[17]

(6) Wealth in the contemporary world is not simply to be found in resources, but rather in ideas, entrepreneurial instincts, skills. The wealth of nations is no longer stuff in the ground; the wealth of nations resides in the human mind, in human creativity.[18]

(7) Poverty in today's circumstances is primarily a matter of exclusion from networks of productivity and

exchange; it is not to be understood simply or simplistically as a matter of having an unequal and inadequate portion of what are imagined to be a fixed number of economic goods. Thus we should think of the poor not as a problem to be solved (as modern social-welfare states tend to do), but as people with potential to be unleashed. Welfare programmes should aim at developing the habits and skills that allow the poor to participate in networks of productivity and exchange.[19]

In his 1993 encyclical on moral theology, *Veritatis splendor*, John Paul II also had important things to say about the free and virtuous society. To take but one example: the Pope's teaching that the equality of citizens before the law is most securely grounded in our common human responsibility to avoid intrinsically evil acts is an intriguing proposal for democratic theory to consider.[20]

Finally, in his 1995 encyclical *Evangelium vitae*, John Paul made his most developed statement on the relationship of constitutional and statutory law to the moral law, and on the relationship of the moral law to the free and virtuous society. Democracies risk self-destruction, the Pope warned, if moral wrongs are defended and promoted as 'rights'. A law-governed democracy is impossible over the long haul when a certain class of citizens claims the right to dispose of other classes of citizens through the private use of lethal violence. Reducing human beings to useful (or useless, or troublesome) objects for manipulation erodes the moral culture that makes democracy possible. Abortion and euthanasia are two examples of this deadly syndrome; the production of so-called 'research embryos' destined from conception for experimentation and death is another. A 'culture of life' is thus essential for democracy and for human flourishing. Unless the State has no other means to defend itself against predatory individuals, the use of capital punishment erodes the culture of life and should thus be avoided.[21]

John Paul's social doctrine has taken the Catholic Church into new territory. There is no sense in these encyclicals of a nostalgia for the world of the *ancien régime*; there is not the slightest hint of a longing for the way things were before the emergence of the modern state and the modern economy. *Centesimus annus*, in particular, brought a new empirical sensitivity to the papal social magisterium, which has at times been characterized by a certain abstractness about political and economic life. A Church widely perceived as a foe of democracy in the nineteenth century has become, through the Second Vatican Council and the social magisterium of John Paul II, perhaps the world's foremost institutional defender of human rights, and a sophisticated participant in the world-wide debate over the nature and functioning of democracy.[22]

Indeed, one can widen the lens ever further and say that, at the turn of the millennium, the social doctrine of the

Church had a comprehensive quality and a salience in public life that would have amazed Leo XIII, 'prisoner of the Vatican'. As the century and the millennium turned, there were three proposals for organizing the human future that had global reach and were supported by the necessary institutional infrastructure to have a world-wide impact. One proposal was the pragmatic utilitarianism that defined much of moral discourse in western Europe and North America, even as it was carried world-wide through American popular culture and certain aspects of economic globalization. The second was the proposal of radical Islam. And the third was the proposal of Catholic social doctrine: a way of living freedom that ties freedom to truth and truth to goodness, and a way of thinking about the human prospect that can be engaged by every person of good will. One does not risk a charge of special pleading by suggesting that the course of the twenty-first century and beyond will be determined in no small part by the answer to the question, how will each of these proposals shape the emerging global culture?

The development of Catholic social doctrine

What, then, is the work that John Paul II has left the rest of us to do as we consider the Church's social doctrine in the first years of a new century and millennium? Let me suggest here a pastoral/catechetical issue, a methodological issue and a set of specific policy issues where the wisdom of Catholic social doctrine is urgently needed, but the social doctrine itself remains, at present, insufficiently developed.

The pastoral/catechetical issue: the reception of social doctrine

The first thing to be done about Catholic social doctrine in the twenty-first century is to ensure that it is far more thoroughly received throughout the world Church.

In the United States, it is often said that Catholic social doctrine is Catholicism's 'best-kept secret'. There is an unfortunate amount of truth in that. The social doctrine of the Church is rarely preached and poorly catechized. It is possible to complete a pre-ordination theology programme without having taken a semester-long course on the Church's social doctrine. Courses in the social doctrine of the Church are rarely a staple of secondary or college-level Catholic education. The social doctrine of the Church is barely mentioned in most programmes that prepare adults for baptism or for reception into full communion with the Church. In all of this, I fear that the Church in the United States is not alone.

The compendium of social doctrine that has been in preparation at the Pontifical Council for Justice and Peace for several years is itself a testimony to the world Church's failure to draw deeply enough from the wells of its own wisdom in the related fields of culture, economics and politics – if the Church had truly received the social doctrine of the twentieth-century popes, would such a compendium be necessary? The pastoral leaders of the Church, including the world episcopate, are simply not as conversant with the Church's social doctrine as they must be if the Catholic proposal is to have the impact it should on shaping the emerging global culture.

This question of reception is both general and specific. In addition to a generalized failure to make the social doctrine 'live' in the local Churches, intellectually and pastorally, there has been a specific failure to reckon with the distinctive contributions of John Paul II to Catholic social teaching. In more than a few Catholic intellectual and activist circles in western Europe, North America and Latin America, it often seems as if *Centesimus annus* had never been written. In these quarters, the quixotic search for a 'Catholic third way' somewhere 'beyond' capitalism and socialism continues apace, and the teaching of *Centesimus annus* on the free economy is virtually ignored. Several interventions at the 2001 Synod of Bishops also suggested a striking unfamiliarity with John Paul II's social doctrine and its emphasis on the poor as people with potential who are to be empowered to enter local, national and international networks of productivity and exchange. 'Globalization' was often discussed in the Synod absent the empirical sensitivity evident in *Centesimus annus*. Indeed, in so far as one purpose of *Centesimus annus* was to challenge dependency theory and other forms of Marxist-influenced economic analysis in Latin American Catholicism, it must be said that the encyclical has, to date, not been altogether successfully received in the new demographic centre of the world Church.

Thus a more thorough reception of the twentieth-century papal social magisterium, with specific reference to the social magisterium of John Paul II, is an imperative for twenty-first-century Catholicism.

The methodological issue: refining principles through rigorously empirical analysis

The world Church owes the Church of western Europe a great debt of gratitude for taking the lead from the mid-nineteenth to the mid-twentieth centuries in developing Catholic social theory in its modern form. That influence continues today, as a glance at the *Annuario pontificio* and the demographics of the relevant organs of the Holy See devoted to social doctrine demonstrates. No serious student of Catholic social doctrine can doubt that those steeped in the intellectual traditions that produced von Ketteler and von Nell-Breuning, Maritain and Simon, and other such giant figures will have much to contribute to the development of Catholic social thought in the twenty-first century.[23]

That continental European legacy must be complemented in the twenty-first century, however, by an intensified dialogue with Catholic social thinking as it has evolved in the United States. I have done no scientific survey of the matter, but I think it not unlikely that the social doctrine of this pontificate has had its greatest public impact in America. Several of the encyclicals cited just above were debated in the secular American press with an interest and rigour that was not always evident in other parts of the world Church; indeed, I think it is fair to say that no great world newspaper has taken this pontificate with such intellectual seriousness as the *Wall Street Journal*, arguably the world's most important business newspaper. A journal that regularly explores the implications of John Paul II's social doctrine, *First Things*, is the most widely read religious–intellectual journal in America, and indeed one of the most widely read intellectual journals, period. In the United States, book-length analyses of Catholic social doctrine are debated in intellectual and public-policy circles far beyond the formal boundaries of the Catholic Church. All this suggests a dynamic ferment of reflection that, in dialogue with its European antecedents, will be important in developing the social doctrine of the Church in the new century.

American Catholic social ethicists and theologians and their colleagues from throughout the Anglosphere will bring to the development of Catholic social doctrine in the twenty-first century an inductive, empirical approach to social analysis that will complement the more deductive, abstract analysis that has characterized continental

European approaches to Catholic social thought. Differing Anglo-Saxon and continental European concepts of human rights and of the nature of law, and differing American and European experiences of the social-welfare state and the management of the free economy, will be put into conversation in ways that should produce a more intellectually rich result.[24]

In discussing briefly this North American–European axis of dialogue, I do not in any way intend to demean the crucial contributions to Catholic social thought that must come from Latin America and from the new Churches of Africa and Asia. I do mean to emphasize what seems to me the more thorough discussion of the social doctrine of John Paul II that has taken place among American Catholic intellectuals, and the importance of that for the world Church of the next decades, in common intellectual work and in the relevant offices in Rome.

Five specific issues

1. Catholic international-relations theory

The events of 9/11 and the response to them throughout the world Church have reminded us that Catholic international-relations theory must be refined and developed if the Church is to bring the moral wisdom of its tradition to the pursuit of the peace of order, justice, and freedom in world affairs. John XXIII's *Pacem in terris* is not usually considered a 'social encyclical' or an integral part of the Church's social doctrine. But here, too, a development of thinking is in order. If the social doctrine of the Church is prepared to address issues of globalization in the economic sphere, it must be prepared to help statesmen and citizens think through the transition from world dis-order to a measure of world order in the sphere of international politics. The 'social question' now includes the question of world order.

The first requirement in this area of intellectual development is, I suggest, to retrieve the classic Catholic notion of peace as *tranquillitas ordinis*: the tranquillity of that 'order' within and among nations that is composed of justice and freedom.[25] In this context, it is also essential to renew our understanding of the just-war tradition as a tradition of statecraft in which all the instruments of legitimate public authority, including the instruments of proportionate and discriminate armed force, are analysed for their ability to contribute to the building of *tranquillitas ordinis* on a global scale. Among many other things, this renewal of understanding will mean recovering the classic structure of the Catholic just-war tradition, which does not begin with a series of means-tests but with a demonstration of legitimate public authority's obligation to defend the innocent and pursue justice. The just-war tradition must, in other words, be renewed as a reflection on obligatory political ends, rather than be further reduced (as it has been in recent decades) to a thin casuistry of means. *Ad bellum* questions must once again take their proper theological priority in moral analysis over *in bello* issues, if the latter are going to be understood properly.

This, in turn, will require a development of the just war tradition itself. How are we to understand the classic components of 'just cause'? Does the first use of military force to prevent the use of a weapon of mass destruction satisfy the classic concept of a 'just cause' as 'repelling aggression'? In order to think through the full implications of the Holy Father's teaching that 'humanitarian intervention' is a moral obligation in the face of impending or actual genocide or mass starvation, is it necessary to recover the older 'just cause' notion of 'punishment for evil' as a legitimate *causus belli*? Questions of 'legitimate authority' are also in need of urgent investigation. Where is the locus of moral legitimacy in world politics today? Are there occasions when military action absent the sanction of the UN Security Council can serve the ends of *tranquillitas ordinis*? What does the *ad bellum* criterion of 'last resort' mean in a world where unstable, aggressive regimes may possess weapons of mass destruction, the means to deliver them over long distances, and the capacity to transfer them to terrorist organizations? Are there circumstances in which 'last resort' can mean 'only' resort, given the nature of the regimes involved? Indeed, does the just-war tradition challenge the Westphalian notion of the sovereign immunity of the nation-state, in itself and in light of the emergence of states which are innately threats to world order because of their ideology and their weapons capabilities?[26]

These are all questions in need of urgent attention. Catholic international-relations theory has lain fallow for the better part of four decades. It is time to revive it and develop it as an important component of the social doctrine of the Church.

2. Interreligious dialogue and the global 'social question'

As I noted a moment ago, activist Islam is one of the other proposals for the human future with global 'reach' in the early part of this new millennium. This suggests that the social doctrine of the Church must take its place in inter-religious dialogue, if that dialogue is to be anything more than an ineffectual exercise in political correctness. This, in turn, suggests that the Catholic–Islamic dialogue in the immediate future must be framed, from the Catholic point of view, in frankly strategic terms.

Can the Catholic Church, in other words, be of some modest assistance to those Islamic scholars, lawyers and religious leaders who are working – often at great risk – to develop a genuinely Islamic case for religious toleration in something approximating what we in the West would call 'civil society'? If a world safe for diversity and pluralism requires a billion Muslims to become good Rawlsian secular liberals, then we really do face the grim prospect of a global 'clash of civilizations'. Thus the crucial question for the Islamic future, from the vantage point of Catholic social doctrine, is whether Islam can find within its sacred texts and legal traditions the *internal* resources to ground an Islamic case for crucial aspects of the free and virtuous society, including religious toleration and a commitment to the method of persuasion in politics.

Some may wonder whether the Catholic Church has anything of particular interest to bring to this discussion. What it has to offer, I suggest, is its own recent history – for it took the Catholic Church until 1965 to develop and articulate a thoroughly *Catholic* concept of religious freedom and its implications for the organization of public life. Indeed, one can draw a rough analogy between pro-civil-society Islamic scholars and religious leaders today and those Catholic intellectuals and bishops who were probing toward some sort of *rapprochement* with religious freedom and democracy as the old order was crumbling in Europe throughout the nineteenth century. Surely there are lessons to be learned from this experience – which eventually led to a dramatic development of social doctrine in Vatican II's Declaration on Religious Freedom (*Dignitatis humanae*) – that could and should be brought into the Catholic Church's global dialogue with the multi-faceted worlds of Islam.

3. The emerging global economy and the environment
Centesimus annus has raised a host of important questions for further exploration. Its phenomenology of economic life suggests the possibility that there are economic 'laws' written into the human condition in a way analogous to the moral law. Teasing out what those 'laws' might be

should be one issue on the agenda of exploration in the years immediately ahead. Important experiments in welfare reform are now under way in various countries; monitoring those experiments in light of *Centesimus annus*'s critique of the 'Social Assistance State', its teaching on poverty-as-exclusion and its endorsement of empowerment strategies for including the poor in networks of productivity and exchange will help develop the social doctrine in the early decades of the century.

The condition of the world's poor is a moral scandal, not least because today, for perhaps the first time in human history, poverty is not necessary, not something fixed in the order of things. The Church thus has an obligation to lift up before the world the moral imperative of eradicating poverty. In doing so, however, Catholic social doctrine and its exponents should focus primary attention on questions of wealth creation rather than wealth distribution. Billions of human beings today are *not* poor, which is a tremendous moral as well as economic achievement. Rigorous empirical analysis of how poverty has been conquered, wealth created and the formerly poor empowered to unleash the economic creativity that is theirs must inform the development of Catholic social doctrine in the twenty-first century. This does not mean exchanging Catholic social doctrine for Adam Smith and *The Wealth of Nations*. The Church must always remind the free economy that there are economic things that can be done but should not be done; it must always remind the free economy that it, too, is under moral scrutiny and that calculations of efficiency are not the only measure of integral human development. But to note, as the social doctrine must, that the tremendous energies unleashed by the free economy must be directed by a vibrant public moral culture and by law does not mean a Church opting for socialism; it means a Church teaching the moral principles essential for the ongoing reform of the free economy.[27]

The emerging social doctrine of the twenty-first century must also address much more directly the problem of corruption as an obstacle to development. A decade ago, Latin America seemed poised on the edge of a genuine breakthrough, politically and economically; now we see the Catholic countries of the Andean region and Argentina in crisis. Both local pastors and knowledgeable observers have said that one major cause of these crises is corruption: corruption in the legal and political systems, and a culture of corruption that distorts individual consciences. Here is perhaps the clearest example of the failure of the Church to 'receive' its own social doctrine. That failure must be reversed if the bright promise of Latin America is to be realized in the century ahead.

Catholic social thinking must also shed some bad intellectual habits if it is to play its essential role in creating a global moral culture capable of disciplining and directing the globalization process. We must stop thinking of the so-called 'gap' between the developed and the underdeveloped as the chief defining characteristic of the world economic situation and ask again, with *Centesimus annus*, how to unleash the potential of the poor so that they can participate in networks of productivity and exchange. We must stop describing failed mercantilist and oligarchic systems in Latin America as failures of 'capitalism'. We must stop thinking of the State as the first (and, to some minds, only) instrument of recourse in resolving problems of poverty, education and health care, and we must encourage individual and corporate philanthropies that support a thick network of voluntary organizations capable of empowering the poor, educating the illiterate and healing the sick; Catholic social doctrine must also encourage the formation of legal and tax systems that encourage philanthropy and support independent-sector initiatives in the fields of health, education and welfare. We must resolve not to make intellectual common cause with the demographic, economic and environmental prophets of doom who see nothing but decay and ruin in the present and the future. Employing the new empirical rigour exemplified by the social magisterium of John Paul II, Catholic social ethicists of the twenty-first century would recognize that life expectancy is increasing on a global basis, including the Third World; that water and air in the developed world are cleaner than in five hundred years; that fears of chemicals poisoning the earth are wildly exaggerated; that both energy and food are cheaper and more plentiful throughout the world than ever before; that 'over-population' is a myth; that the global picture is, in truth, one of unprecedented human prosperity – and, recognizing these facts,

Catholic social ethicists would ask, as I have suggested above, why? What creates wealth and distributes it broadly? What are the systemic political, economic and cultural factors that have created this unprecedented prosperity, which is not (contrary to the shibboleths) limited to a shrinking, privileged elite? What can be done to make this prosperity even more broadly available?[28]

Finally, in this regard, Catholic social doctrine must follow through on the suggestion of *Centesimus annus* that the spiritual challenge of a time of rising abundance will be to understand and live the truth that, while there is nothing inherently wrong with wanting to have more material goods, there is something morally wrong (and, ultimately, economically destructive) about imagining that *having more* is *being more*. The Church must, in other words, develop and inculcate a spirituality for abundance, in which the solipsism and selfishness too often characteristic of certain developed societies (and manifest, for example, in their demographic suicide) is challenged by the call to a rich generosity.

4. The life issues as social-doctrine issues

The new genetic knowledge and the biotechnologies to which it has given rise offer immense possibilities for healing and enriching human life; they also open the prospect of humanity sliding into a brave new world of manufactured and stunted human beings. Because the biotechnology challenge is, in no small part, a matter of public policy, the life issues must be seen in the twenty-first century as a crucial set of questions for Catholic social doctrine as well as for bioethics *stricte dictu*.

Here, perhaps the most urgent need at the moment is for a development and elaboration of the Catholic theory of democracy. In *Centesimus annus*, John Paul II alerted the world to the dangers inherent in a purely instrumental view of democratic governance. In *Veritatis splendor*, he suggested that a robust public moral culture, recognizing the moral truths inscribed in the human condition, is essential in defending such bedrock democratic principles as equality-before-the-law, as well as in managing passions and interests, fighting corruption and maintaining democratic 'inclusiveness'. In *Evangelium vitae*, the Pope illustrated precisely how abortion and euthanasia, by placing certain classes of human beings outside the protection of the law, threaten the very moral structure of the democratic project. Now is the time to develop these insights into a public moral vocabulary capable of challenging the rampant utilitarianism that dominates debates on these questions today.

To take one important example: Catholic social doctrine proposes a 'dignitarian' view of the human person and challenges certain biotechological procedures, including cloning, on the moral ground that they violate the innate 'human dignity' of persons. What, precisely, is the content of that 'human dignity'? What are its component parts? How is it violated by certain practices? What are the consequences for democracy of these violations? John Paul II has given us a supple, rigorous framework for reflection on these questions. It is imperative that we begin to fill in that framework in order to shift the terms of the public moral debate.

For more than two decades now, the Church in the United States, the United Kingdom and indeed throughout the world has argued that abortion is not a question of sexual morality but of public justice: a question of the fifth commandment, not the sixth. In the decades ahead, and with the biotechnology challenge compounding the challenge of the abortion licence and euthanasia, Catholic social doctrine must demonstrate ever more specifically and persuasively how the protection of innocent life is a first principle of justice without which democracy will self-destruct. We must, in other words, demonstrate ever more persuasively that the life issues are *public* issues with immense *public* consequences, and not simply matters of individual 'choice'. Doing that will require a richer, thicker Catholic theory of democracy.

5. The 'priority of culture' and the deepening of civil society

In one respect, *Centesimus annus* marked an official recognition by the papal magisterium that the two great structural questions that had agitated the world since the industrial and French revolutions had been settled – by history. If, under the conditions of modernity (urbanization, mass literacy, industrialization and post-industrialization) one wants a society that protects human rights while advancing the common good and permitting participation in government, one chooses democracy over the *ancien régime*, or its fascist or communist alternatives. If one wants a growing economy that enables the exercise of economic initiative, fosters participation, increases wealth and spreads it widely, one chooses a market-centred economy over a state-centred economy. These mega-questions of political and economic structure have been settled. But while much of the world may have thought that those were the only real questions at issue, John Paul II and the social doctrine of the Church read the present and the future more insightfully. What remains, the Pope proposed in *Centesimus annus*, are the truly urgent questions: the questions of public moral culture and civil society, which will determine whether those well-functioning machines, democracy and the market, continue to function well.

The formation of men and women capable of leading free political communities and managing free economies so that freedom serves human flourishing is thus another urgent question for the social doctrine of the Church in the decades immediately ahead. Catholic democratic theory has, in the main, focused on structural questions of participation, representation, voting rights, the rights of association, and so forth. With these questions largely resolved, the focus must now be on 'the priority of culture': on the institutions of civil society and their capacity to form genuine democrats. As already indicated just above, this will require urgent attention in the immediate future to the problem of corruption and the essentials of integrity in public life. John Paul II's suggestive phrase, the 'subjectivity of society', must be filled in with a more thorough analysis of the institutions of civil society and their relationship to the structures of the democratic state and the free economy.

This discussion should include a re-examination of the way in which many trade unions currently function. There is no question that the right of worker association is well established in Catholic social doctrine and will remain so. It is also indisputable that in certain advanced societies, unions are now a reactionary economic and political force, impeding necessary economic change and functioning as narrow interest groups rather than as elements of the 'subjectivity of society' with a profound concern for the common good. The fierce resistance of American teachers' unions to any notion of empowering poor children through the provision of vouchers or tax credits, enabling them to escape failing public (and union-dominated) government-run schools in order to attend independent (often Catholic) schools, is a case in point. Examples of similar union-based resistance to economic change in Europe could be multiplied exponentially. That a union must defend its own goes without saying; when a union defends *only* its own, to the manifest detriment of the rest of society (and especially the poor), something is seriously

awry. Catholic social doctrine needs to rethink the nature
and role of unions in the post-industrial economy and in
modern democracy.

A concluding, and decidedly unscientific, postscript

Francis Fukuyama discerned a paradox at the heart of
modern society that touches directly on the challenge of
'the priority of culture' to Catholic social doctrine:

> If the institutions of democracy and capitalism are to
> work properly, they must co-exist with certain pre-
> modern cultural habits that ensure their proper
> functioning. Law, contract, and economic rationality
> provide a necessary but not sufficient basis for both
> the stability and prosperity of postindustrial societies;
> they must as well be leavened with reciprocity, moral
> obligation, duty toward community, and trust, which
> are based in habit rather than rational calculation.
> The latter are not anachronisms in a modern society
> but rather the sine qua non of the latter's success.[29]

A Church that recognizes the 'priority of culture' in the
postmodern circumstances of the twenty-first century,
and whose social doctrine addresses postmodern society at
this depth level of its self-understanding, is positioned

squarely on the leading edge of the debate over the future of freedom. Far from being left on the margins, such a Church may find itself, at times, disturbingly 'relevant'. But that, too, is one of the challenges facing Catholic social doctrine in the decades ahead.

Notes

1   The text of the *Letter to Diognetus* may be found in *The Apostolic Fathers*, 2nd edn, trans. J. B. Lightfoot and J. R. Hammer, ed. and rev. by Michael W. Holmes (Grand Rapids, MI: Baker, 1989), pp. 296–306. *Lumen gentium* cited *Diognetus* in describing the Christian's place in 'the world' (cf. *Lumen gentium* 38), while the *Catechism of the Catholic Church* (at 2240) cites *Diognetus* on the duties of Christian citizens. For a fuller discussion of the Diognetian perspective on being 'the Church in the world', see my essay, 'What the Church asks of the world, or, Diognetus revisited', in *Soul of the World: Notes on the Future of Public Catholicism* (Grand Rapids, MI: Eerdmans, 1996), pp. 31–46.

2   Hans Urs von Balthasar, *Truth Is Symphonic: Aspects of Christian Pluralism* (San Francisco, CA: Ignatius Press, 1987), p. 87.

3   H. Richard Niebuhr, *Christ and Culture* (New York: Harper & Row, 1956).

4   For a fuller analysis of the principle of subsidiarity, see my essay, 'Catholicism and democracy: the other twentieth century revolution', in *Soul of the World*, pp. 107–10.

5   This experience of a nascent civil society was critically important in the collapse of European communism; the emergence of a resistance community as an alternative form of civil society to communist fakery was brilliantly analysed by several key figures in the resistance. See, for example, Václav Havel, 'The power of the powerless', and Václav Benda, 'Catholicism and politics', in Havel *et al.*, *The Power of the Powerless* (Armonk, NY: M. E. Sharpe, Inc. 1990), and Józef Tischner, *The Spirit of Solidarity* (San Francisco, CA: Harper & Row, 1982). See also Jacques Maritain, *Christianity and Democracy* (San Francisco, CA: Ignatius Press, 1986).

6   John Paul II, *Laborem exercens*, 4, 25.

7   *ibid.*, 6.

8   *ibid.*, 25–7.

9   John Paul II, *Sollicitudo rei socialis*, 15.

10 *ibid.*, 15–16, 45.

11 *ibid.*, 28.

12 *ibid.*, 16–17.

13 John Paul II, *Centesimus annus*, 42, 51.

14 *ibid.*, 46.

15 *ibid.*, 44–52.

16 *ibid.*, 42.

17 *ibid.*, 13, 46, 49.

18 *ibid.*, 32.

19 *ibid.*, 58, 52. For further discussion, see Richard John Neuhaus, *Doing Well and Doing Good: The Challenge to the Christian Capitalist* (New York: Doubleday, 1992), especially Chapter 8, 'The potential of the poor'.

20 John Paul II, *Veritatis splendor*, 96.

21 John Paul II, *Evangelium vitae*, 20, 18, 56.

22 For a fuller account of this evolution, see my essay, 'Catholicism and democracy: the other twentieth century revolution'.

23 For a brilliantly concise survey of the European intellectual foundations of Catholic social doctrine, see Franz H. Mueller, *The Church and the Social Question* (Washington, DC: American Enterprise Institute, 1984).

24 For one example of this process at work, see Mary Ann Glendon, *Rights Talk* (New York: Free Press, 1993).

25 St Augustine provides this definition of 'peace' in *The City of God*, xix, 13. For discussion of the evolution of this idea, its abandonment in recent years, and intellectuals' steps towards its resuscitation, see my *Tranquillitas Ordinis: The Present Failure and Future Promise of American Catholic Thought on War and Peace* (New York: Oxford University Press, 1987).

26 For a deeper probe into these questions, see my essay, 'Moral clarity in a time of war', *First Things* 129 (January 2003), pp. 20–7.

27 On these points, see William McGurn, 'Pulpit economics', *First Things* 122 (April 2002), pp. 21–5

28 A remarkable book by a Danish statistician, Bjørn Lomborg, should be required reading for all those interested in developing Catholic social thought in the decades ahead. Not only does Lomborg (a lifelong Green and man of the Left) provide an ocean of data refuting the environmental and economic prophets of gloom, he does so in a way that does not ignore, but rather engages with great moral earnestness, the genuine questions of choice that have to be made in concretizing our commitments to empowering the poor and preserving and enhancing the environment. See Lomborg, *The Skeptical Environmentalist: Measuring the Real State of the* World (Cambridge: Cambridge University Press, 2001).

29 Francis Fukuyama, *Trust: The Social Virtues and the Creation of Prosperity* (New York: The Free Press, 1995), p. 11. See also my essay, 'Capitalism for humans', *Commentary*, October 1995, pp. 34–8.

Notes on Contributors

Charles Moore was educated at Trinity College, Cambridge (BA Hons. History). He was a leader writer and then an assistant editor and political columnist. In 1983 he began working for the *Spectator* and the following year became its editor, a post he retained until 1990. In 1987 he became a weekly columnist for the *Daily Express* and then Deputy Editor of the *Telegraph* in 1990. Two years later he became the Editor of the *Sunday Telegraph*, a position he held until 1995 when he finally became Editor of the *Daily Telegraph*, leaving in 2003 to work on his authorized biography of Margaret Thatcher.

Gyles Brandreth. A former Oxford scholar, President of the Oxford Union and MP for the City of Chester, Gyles Brandreth's varied career has ranged from being a Whip and Lord Commissioner of the Treasury in John Major's government to starring in his own award-winning musical revue in London's West End. A prolific broadcaster, an acclaimed interviewer (principally for the *Sunday Telegraph*), novelist, children's author and biographer, his best-selling diary, *Breaking the Code*, was described by *The Times* as 'By far the best political diary of recent years, far more perceptive and revealing than Alan Clark's.' For 25 years he has been involved in the work of the National Playing Fields Association, whose Patron is the Queen and whose President is the Duke of Edinburgh. His most recent book is the best-selling royal biography, *Philip & Elizabeth: Portrait of a Marriage* (Century, 2004). His account of his first visit to the Tyburn Convent is published in *Brief Encounters: Meetings with Remarkable People* (Politico's Paperbacks, 2004).

Cherie Booth practises in employment and discrimination law. In her public law practice she advises local authorities and other public bodies, and individuals and companies. She lectures widely in the UK and abroad on human rights and advises on the implications of the Human Rights Act. She sits as a recorder in the County Court and Crown Court and is a bencher of Lincoln's Inn. Her book *The Goldfish Bowl: Married to the Prime Minister* was published by Random House in 2004.

George Weigel is the author of 13 books, and is best known internationally for his biography of Pope John Paul II, *Witness to Hope*. Published in 1999 in English, French, Italian and Spanish, *Witness to Hope* has subsequently appeared in Polish, Portuguese, Slovak, Czech, Slovenian, Russian and German. Mr Weigel has contributed articles to opinion journals and newspapers throughout the world and is a consultant on Vatican Affairs for NBC News. His weekly column, 'The Catholic Difference', is syndicated to 60 newspapers in the United States.

Adorers of the Sacred Heart of Jesus of Montmartre OSB

Tyburn Convent, 8 Hyde Park Place, London W2 2LJ

Tel: 020 7723 7262
Fax: 020 7706 4507
Website: www.tyburnconvent.org.uk

The convent at Tyburn

The high-profile annual Tyburn lecture was inaugurated in 2001 by Tyburn Nuns at their London convent to provide a platform for national and international figures to speak on their choice of a contemporary topic.

Tyburn Convent is the home of the Tyburn Nuns, The Adorers of the Sacred Heart of Jesus of Montmartre, Order of St Benedict.

They pray night and day before the Blessed Sacrament to honour the 105 Catholic martyrs who suffered and died for their faith on the scaffold of Tyburn Tree between 1535 and 1681. They also pray continuously for the needs of all mankind, especially for the people of Great Britain.